MIRACLE in DARIEN

Bob Slosser

Logos International
Plainfield, New Jersey

All Scripture references, unless otherwise noted,
are taken from the Revised Standard Version
of the Bible.

For my wife and children

God seems first to find His man or woman, and second to lay out a set of principles for the people, and then to say, "Now work them out."

Bob Slosser

Contents

PART ONE:

THE MAN

CHAPTER ONE

Mount Sinai

On the third new moon after the people of Israel had gone forth out of the land of Egypt, on that day they came into the wilderness of Sinai. And when they set out from Rephidim and came into the wilderness of Sinai, they encamped in the wilderness; and there Israel encamped before the mountain. And Moses went up to God, and the Lord called to him out of the mountain.[1]

It was the middle of the night. Suddenly Terry was wide awake, listening to the silence. It was powerful in its totality, as though a giant, transparent shield covered the universe, creating a vacuum of sound. Terry soon realized he wasn't breathing; the stillness seemed to stop all bodily movements. He took a deep breath, and exhaled. He was still alive.

He climbed out of bed, his bare feet maintaining the silence as they moved across the wooden floor and out onto the balcony just off his room. His breathing stopped again. He had never seen so many stars; they seemed to burst from the heavens, millions of them, in every part of the sky. And the August night was gently warm, still but warm, even though the sky looked cold in its brilliance.

---

[1]Exodus 19:1-3.

"I'm miles and miles from any place." His low voice split the silence. "It's like the middle of the desert."

But it wasn't just a desert. It was Mount Sinai. There it was, in front of him; it, too, incredibly still. The peaks were staggering—stark, slashing the starlight, overpowering in their dark massiveness.

Terry was at the foot of Jebel Musa, accepted by tradition and most modern scholars as Mount Sinai, where in the third month after the Israelites' departure from Egypt, God revealed himself and gave the Ten Commandments and other laws to Moses. Situated at the southern end of a two-mile ridge of granite, its sheer formations were awesome, rising to a height of 7,363 feet.

He was standing on a balcony of the Monastery of St. Catherine at the foot of the mountain, also known in the Old Testament as Horeb. His mind raced as his eyes swept back and forth, up and down, over the rugged terrain.

"What time is it?" he thought, and he raised his wristwatch in front of his face. Its dial shone in the dark. "Ten minutes till twelve." In three hours and ten minutes he'd be getting ready for the climb to the top of the mountain. It was August and they'd have to start early to get to the top before the heat reached the blistering stage. The first three hours would be on camelback; after that he'd be climbing and crawling over those massive outcroppings of rock.

As he stood in the starlit silence, his mind was flooded with thoughts of Moses, the wilderness wanderings, Sinai, the Commandments. God had spoken at this very place, assuming tradition was correct in pinpointing this as Mount Sinai. Terry, an Episcopal priest and college professor from Rhode Island, was nearing the end of a summer project for the Israeli government, retracing the route of the Israelites as they had fled from Egypt, as

4

recorded in the Old Testament. He had been virtually living in Exodus, Numbers, and Deuteronomy. Moses was very real to him.

Standing on the balcony in his pajamas, barefoot, his black, wavy hair stirring ever so slightly in the gentle breeze, he knew something extraordinary was happening.

"Lord, are you saying something to me?" he whispered into the night. "What is it, Lord?"

An Unexpected Call

Everett L. Fullam—Terry to all who knew him—had left the United States nearly two months earlier, at the beginning of the summer of 1972, happily pursuing his ivory tower life. He had been ordained an Episcopal priest at the age of thirty-six, but had continued his busy life as scholar, academician, and musician, showing no inclination toward the parish priesthood beyond occasional teaching missions. He had frequently been asked to consider calls to churches, but had consistently turned them down without a second thought. He, his wife, Ruth, and their three children were perfectly suited to their life at Barrington College in Rhode Island. Biblical studies, philosophy, logic—they were right up his alley, as was the opportunity to spend the summer traveling and studying in Israel.

But then had come that unexpected call shortly before he was to leave for the Middle East.

"Hello. Father Fullam?" The voice was deep and masculine.

"Yes."

"This is Reg Jones down at St. Paul's, Darien," the deep, slowly paced voice said.

Terry thought for a moment. He had taught on two occasions at St. Paul's Episcopal Church in Darien,

Connecticut, a wealthy coastal town forty-five minutes north of New York City. That was Art Lane's church. It was an unusual place. Reg Jones was the senior warden, a nice guy.

"Oh, yes. Hello, Reg. It's good to hear your voice again."

"Same here," Jones said.

Several seconds passed in silence. Then Jones continued. "Terry, the vestry's just been told that Art Lane's resigning. He's going up to Cape Cod—to the Community of Jesus."

"Is that right?" Fullam said slowly. "That's a surprise, isn't it?"

"Yes," Jones replied. "The church hasn't even been told yet. They'll get a letter this week."

Again, a pause.

"I'm calling to ask you to consider coming here," Jones said at last.

Silence. He went ahead, "You seemed to pop into everybody's mind at once when Art told us. Most of them said we were out of our minds, when your name was raised. 'He'd never even think of such a thing,' they said."

Fullam laughed. "They're pretty close to right," he said, but then he hesitated.

Jones jumped in. "Well, won't you at least consider it?"

Fullam opened his mouth to say no, but he hesitated again. Then to his surprise, he said, "Yes, I'll consider it."

He couldn't believe he'd said it. It was completely contrary to his instincts. "This is ridiculous," he said to himself—and something seemed to be trying to push itself into his consciousness—but aloud he spoke into the telephone, "You know, I'm leaving for Israel in a little over a week, and I'll be gone all summer."

Jones didn't stop for a second. "Well, we'll have to get you down here soon then, before you go."

Fullam chuckled. "This is ridiculous," he said again to himself. What was it he was trying to remember? "Why don't I just tell him right now I know I won't come? Why not save all the bother?" But, again, he spoke contrarily when he opened his mouth. "Okay, if you can arrange it. I'll come down and see your calling committee."

Three days passed, and Terry and Ruth were in Darien, sitting in Reg and Judy Jones's home with nearly twenty people from the church. Ruth was very quiet. Terry was ready to be questioned, but no one seemed to have anything to ask. It appeared quite a few had already made up their minds. He himself had written out a hundred questions he wanted to raise and, when no one was forthcoming, he asked the first one: "If this church were to disappear tomorrow, would anybody miss it?"

A ton of silence fell on the room. No one breathed; all looked straight ahead for several seconds. Then they began to look at one another, seemingly embarrassed. Finally someone said, "Probably not much."

Sensing their embarrassment, Fullam moved on. "Do you really want to be a church, or are you actually looking for a chaplain for your club?"

More silence.

Fullam quickened the tempo, moving on to each phase of the church's ministry and purpose, one question after another. Some elicited answers; some did not. He didn't bother with all one hundred; his point was made.

Some of the men and women in the room were obviously offended, but most were impressed. Several smiled sheepishly, first into their laps and then to one another. They hadn't expected such an inquisition, and they hadn't reckoned on the freedom that Terry enjoyed since he truly wasn't seeking any position. He wasn't bent on pleasing anyone in particular.

As the meeting concluded, Jones asked, "Can you come

down again in two days to meet with the vestry?"

Fullam, rising to his full six-foot-three, two-hundred-twenty-pound stature as he prepared to leave, spoke humbly, "Sure, I'll come down again if you want me to, but then I'll be heading on to Israel."

Two days later he and Ruth drove once again to the proud little town of Darien, and the majority of the vestry at St. Paul's seemed agreed that they wanted to issue a formal call to him. But before he left, he spoke carefully to Jones: "Reg, there's one thing that I insist on, but I don't want you to tell anyone else. I won't even consider coming to this church unless there is a totally unanimous vote. I believe that God can move in unity, but I don't want the calling committee or the vestry to know this; I want God to bring them to one accord."

Jones's face sagged, and for a second he looked like a confused basset hound rather than a confident, urbane, clever accounting executive. "But Terry," he objected, "that'll throw the whole thing out. Nothing has ever been unanimous in this church."

"I can't help it, Reg," Terry said, smiling. "If Jesus is really the head of the church, He's capable of bringing them into accord if this is His will."

Terry flew off for Tel Aviv from Kennedy International Airport two days later, leaving Ruth and the children to a quiet summer by themselves as he studied and ministered. He was quite certain he would remain a college professor.

Preparation in Israel

Above all things, Terry Fullam was a man of the Scriptures. One could almost say he had been born with a Bible in his hand. His mother, a marvelous, twinkly eyed woman who in her later years looked enough like Corrie ten Boom to be her twin sister, often told how Terry, as a

8

little boy, would keep his night light burning into the late hours as he pored over his Bible. And questions and debates about the Scripture and its themes flowed among the closely knit family whenever it was together.

So it seemed natural that as Fullam prayed and thought about his future and St. Paul's Church he began to find his first signs in the Bible. The signs appeared as he moved about the Holy Land, following his lifelong habit of delving into the Scriptures without fail each morning and evening.

The first instruction came in 2 Chronicles 15, a passage dealing with one of the lowest points in the history of the people of God. They had turned away from the Lord; they had forgotten the call that was upon them; indeed, they no longer recognized themselves as the people of God.

Terry read on. There was verse 3: "For a long time Israel was without the true God, and without a teaching priest, and without law." Terry looked up, and then back at the page—*without a teaching priest*. He had never noticed that phrase. His mind whirled. "A teacher I know about, and the priesthood is something I have some understanding of, but what was the function of a teaching priest? What was it Israel needed?"

Sitting quietly for several seconds, he began to understand, and his perceptions deepened as he thought about it then and in the hours following. The Israelites had needed to hear the word of the living God clearly again. They needed to understand that they were a people called out for a special purpose, that they were God's own people. They needed to know that they had a destiny to fulfill, that they had a God who could lead them through everything to accomplish His purpose and will. And so God raised up certain persons and equipped them with a gift of ministry and teaching, igniting them with a vision of His purpose. And Israel was raised out of its despondency. The teaching priest had been the key.

"Thank you, Lord," Terry muttered as he saw the full picture.

Then came Malachi 2, where he was reading along normally until he came to verse 7: "For the lips of a priest should guard knowledge, and men should seek instruction from his mouth, for he is the messenger of the Lord of hosts."

Once again, here was teaching he could understand, but his understanding was pretty much confined to the teaching that took place in a structured environment, in a classroom, where students attended because they wanted to or, at the very least, because they had to. As that kind of a teacher, he knew what he was doing. He knew his material, and he knew how to put it across—he was a logician, among other things. But here was something different. Here, the prophet was saying that the priest was to stand before a congregation and lead it into the will and purpose of almighty God; the priest was the *messenger* of the Lord, the messenger of a *speaking* God.

Putting his Bible down, Terry began to pray and meditate over what he had read. "Father, is it true today, in the middle of the twentieth century, that you still speak your word through individuals?" He had been a so-called charismatic Christian for ten years, believed fully in the miraculous manifestations of the Holy Spirit, and yet had not thought in the terms of Malachi regarding the priesthood and the leading of God's people.

He continued to pray, "Is it still true that people can hear your voice through the ever-so-limited and fallible voice of a human being?"

And at that moment, he knew the Lord spoke back to him: "It is still true."

Everything stopped for several seconds, then his mind

began to whirl again. "But what would I say—how would I know what to say? If it were philosophy, I could teach—Plato, Aristotle, all the others. But how could I do this?"

Before long, he found himself in Jeremiah 23, a strong passage against false shepherds and prophets. He reached verse 16: "Do not listen to the words of the prophets who prophesy to you, filling you with vain hopes; they speak visions of their own minds, not from the mouth of the Lord."

He stopped for a moment. "What was wrong with those people?" He spoke half-aloud. "Exactly what were they doing wrong?"

Then he read on, and verse 18 exploded before him: "For who among them has stood in the council of the Lord to perceive and to hear his word, or who has given heed to his word and listened?"

The light went on brightly for Terry. Those people couldn't speak the word of the Lord because they had not *heard* the word of the Lord. It didn't depend on intelligence or the lack of it. It didn't depend on talents the priest might have. It depended on a willingness to listen, to stand in God's council, to strive to hear and perceive His word.

His eyes went back to his Bible, to verse 22 of that powerful twenty-third chapter of Jeremiah: "But if they had stood in my council, then they would have proclaimed my words to my people, and they would have turned them from their evil way, and from the evil of their doings."

It was necessary for them not only to hear God, but also to speak forth what they heard.

"I Want to Do a New Thing"

"What is it, Lord?" Terry spoke the question into the Sinai darkness. Alone, in the middle of the night, at the foot of the mountain where God had spoken to Moses so many centuries earlier, he was unprepared for what followed.

"You are to go to that church, for I have chosen that congregation to do a mighty work for my name's sake."

Fullam had never had a vision. He had not been blessed with especially supernatural hàppenings; God had always seemed to work supernaturally with him in quite natural ways. In fact, he had clearly heard the voice of the Lord only once in his life—and that was when he was eighteen. But this was unmistakably the voice of the Lord. He had no question about it. He held his breath for a moment. He had really heard the voice. But how? Not with his own ears. He wondered if anyone else would have heard it.

It continued, in a very ordinary, conversational way: "And you are to know that you will never be the head of that church. I am to be the head of that church. And you are to listen. And you are to teach the people to listen. For surely I can guide you where I want you to go."

Terry nodded his head, almost imperceptibly. He was hardly aware of it, but the words slipped from his lips, "Yes, Lord."

The voice, presumably inside him, in his mind, went on, almost eagerly. "I want to do a new thing. It's not the same thing I have done elsewhere. I want to move in a powerful way in that church. It will not be like other churches. Don't put your eyes upon another church and try to copy its program. That is not my plan."

There was a pause, and Terry looked at the massiveness of Mount Sinai and then back toward the plain. The Israelites had camped on that plain, in front of the mountain. Haltingly, he began his part of the conversation.

"Can this really be?" he thought, and then spoke, "Lord, you know I don't have the qualities of a rector; I've never wanted to lead a church."

"Never forget that you are not to be the head of that church," came the reply, a repetition. "I am the head of that church. These are my people and my body and I will direct it as I will direct you."

Terry understood this; he fully believed in the body of Christ principles, and had even taught on them, although he had never seen a church where they were fully carried out. But he understood, and he began to relax and become more conversational himself.

"But Lord," he said, "what about the condition of those people at St. Paul's?"

He was a musician and choirmaster, and his mind went immediately to the choir and something the retiring rector had said: "They sing beautifully, but so far as I can tell, they have no heart for the Lord, only for music." He looked into the darkness and said, "What about that, Lord? What about the choir?"

Clearly and quickly came the response: "I'm going to change them, every one of them."

He heard the statement as plainly as he'd ever heard anything. Without hesitating, he pressed on. "Lord, every vestry I've seen has some committed people, some half-committed, and a lot of uncommitted people."

The answer came before he could ask the question. "I'll change their hearts."

"But what about the congregation, Lord? Surely they're just like every other congregation—a few deeply committed, a circle of people who are committed to the church but not so much to you, and then an outer rim who come unless they have something better to do. What about them, Lord?"

The answer was as clear as the others. "I'm going to change them, from altar to window and wall to wall." His mind flashed back to the sanctuary at St. Paul's; a huge window took up much of the rear wall.

This time the answer didn't stop there. "Don't worry. Not everyone will be ready to move forward, and that's all right. Not everyone will be able to hear at this time, and that's all right. Move forward with the ones I give you. Not even I was able to minister to everybody when I was on earth, and surely you will not. So if people choose to go elsewhere and join in other congregations, let them go, with your blessing. Recognize that I have not written them off, that I can use them in another way and in another place. But your heart and mind is to be single toward me, and then I will do my will in that congregation."

Terry's hand trembled ever so slightly as he raised it toward his face. He had not known such an encounter was possible—but it wasn't over.

"I have chosen that congregation to place my name there in a special sense, and I'm going to do a work there that will be of such a dimension and such a proportion that the wider church will have to take notice of it, because you will be an instrument in my hand to affect the wider church."

This was too much. How could it be? Terry began to voice his reservations. "Lord, why St. Paul's? Why that little congregation? And why me?"

He could almost sense a chuckle in the voice. "It's not because you're particularly special, certainly not that you're better than anybody else."

The words seemed to trail off there, but the thoughts continued, and Terry began to articulate the rest of the response himself. "It's locked up in the mystery of God's sovereign purpose," he said. "There are things that can't be explained, and that's one of them. Why did God take a man from Ur named Abram and found a new race of people in him? Why did He move him out of that land into a new land that he should one day possess? Why did God take a shepherd boy and make him king? Why did the Lord Jesus choose twelve men, none of whom most of us would have chosen if we were starting a new enterprise, and with them set out to renew the face of the whole earth? I don't know the answers. But this seems to be in the character of God. He's done it before."

The conversation appeared to be ended. But Terry's thoughts tumbled onward. He brushed his right hand across his hair. "The most important thing is to establish the headship of Christ over them because the church is His body," he said softly. "He can do nothing until His headship is recognized. And then He'll do it all."

He turned and walked back toward his bed. He nodded his head several times. "God's purpose from the Garden of Eden onward has always been to find a people who will voluntarily respond to Him and move under His leading."

He climbed into bed, glancing at his wristwatch. Nearly an hour had passed since he woke. The most significant change in his forty-two years had taken place in less than sixty minutes.

CHAPTER TWO

A Visit

I picked up the chamber of commerce brochure. "Darien welcomes you for gracious living," the cover said. I opened it and read the first paragraph:

> Darien is a gracious residential community of 22,000 people, nestled between Norwalk and Stamford in Southwestern Connecticut on Long Island Sound, about 45 minutes from New York City. Darien has quick access to the Connecticut Turnpike and the Merritt Parkway. It is located along the historical Boston Post Road. The Penn Central Railroad has two stations with frequent trains to New York. . . .

Further along in the off-white, nicely printed promotion piece, I learned that the town had been established by charter from the state General Assembly in 1820 and prior to that had been part of Stamford, now on the west. The whole thing had been purchased from the Indians in 1640. The earliest settlements were near the mouth of the Noroton River.

In conclusion, the brochure described Darien as a "modern suburban and commuter community with no industry or manufacturing but a growing number of office facilities . . . noted for its dependable and varied hometown stores now mostly in three convenient shopping centers."

Understandably, it did *not* say that the peaceful little community had become noted several years earlier as the setting for a popular novel and motion picture, *Gentleman's Agreement*, revealing deep-rooted and insidious anti-Semitism.

I thought it might help to seek another view, so I turned to an old friend who had lived there for several years. Mike McManus, a former Washington correspondent for *Time* magazine, is an economic and political consultant with a sharp eye for detail, enhanced by an uninterrupted view of his environment from a startling six-foot-seven height. He had finished work on an article about St. Paul's Church for *The Episcopalian* magazine and immediately provided a most significant fact about what he termed "this lush suburb": The average home was selling for $129,000 and prices were still climbing.

"It's not a town of old wealth," he said, "not like Greenwich, ten miles down the line toward New York. But its people, a lot of them anyway, have *made it* in corporate America."

He explained that those sleek, new commuter trains I'd caught a glimpse of on my way in carried twenty-two hundred people into high-paying jobs in Manhattan each day. That's a higher percentage of commuters than in any other town in Connecticut. "Furthermore," he said, "thousands of others travel shorter distances to the headquarters of such firms as IBM, Xerox, General Foods, Olin, and GTE, which have built new suburban corporate headquarters."

Based on my earlier rather sketchy knowledge of that part of southern Connecticut—the affluence of Fairfield

County was nationally known—I could see that Mike was driving toward the truly exceptional and significant factor about Darien, Connecticut: the people. They were professionals—urbane, sophisticated, highly educated, the ones an earlier age would have described as "the pretty people."

As Mike said, "These people are blessed with interesting work, high incomes, and many recreational opportunities."

They threw themselves into highly charged work-lives five days a week from early morning to late evening and then on the weekends turned with equal gusto to a rousing social life that often included participation in one of six private clubs for golf, sailing, riding, swimming, tennis, and just plain wining and dining.

In the world's terms, they were a blessed people.

I drove along the historic Boston Post Road, that 235-mile highway running from New York to Boston which traced its origin to the Old Post Road of colonial days. Its elegance somehow didn't match its name. "Route 1," its official designation, was a little more realistic. The commercial life of much of the town seemed to cling to it, and some of the shops were obviously of high quality.

I turned left onto Mansfield Avenue, one of the few streets I knew from the past, and in a few minutes was into a residential area. A few tentative probes into side streets soon showed that Mike McManus and other writers were correct. It did seem to be an "affluent, sophisticated, quiet town of colonial houses buried in trees, and surrounded by well-clipped expanses of lawn."

The New York Times, CBS, NBC, the *Saturday Review, National Courier*, and numerous others had sent people to check this out. In one way or another, their reporters had been told to "go find out what's going on up there" as word about "that church" had filtered out and across the land, and the oceans, too. "What's happening to those people?" That was the main question. "They've got the world by the tail and yet they're becoming a bunch of religious fanatics." That was the main description.

As I continued out Mansfield Avenue toward the Merritt Parkway and the lovely little town of New Canaan, the bad joke I'd heard kept playing on my lips. It was a one-line take-off on the biblical quotation about Jesus and His hometown of Nazareth: "Can anything good come out of Darien?"

But it wasn't just Darien. All those pretty, rich, New England towns were being affected—New Canaan, Stamford, Westport, Wilton, Ridgefield, and even some over in New York's prestigious Westchester County.

I modified the one-liner as I stared at one particularly beautiful estate set back off the road. The main house was tastefully white, not gaudy in any way, but elegant, quietly expensive. "Lord, you came to preach good news to the poor. How can you do anything in a place like this?"

In about five seconds, I answered myself. "The poor rich are just as poor as the poor poor."

It sounded funny as I said it aloud.

There was the church, on the left, a bit more than two hundred feet off the road. The driveway circled it. The A-frame sanctuary—wood, glass, and some cement block, all looking quite natural in the rustic environment— struck one at first glance as just what it was: the centerpiece of a contemporary Episcopal church. Dozens similar to it could be found around the country. A long, low building set into the contour of the land ran off to the left as one faced it, providing two floors of rooms and offices. There seemed to be very little special about it. Most people would probably describe it merely as "nice."

It was easy to see why the media representatives were baffled. I could almost hear them say, "What is all the fuss about? It's just a plain, little church." But reading their reports, one knew immediately that they had found something they weren't used to. They didn't describe it particularly accurately—in fact, some of them threw a few barbs—but they at least had perceived something worthy of discussing in national news outlets.

Some of them said many of the people of this "affluent community"—almost all of them used that phrase—had "found" religion: primitive, fundamental religion. Some threw around words like "evangelical, born again, charismatic," and some looked for things to poke fun at. Others were obviously impressed with the quality of life they found in these "religious" people of the late twentieth century; one or two indicated that their personal lives had been touched by what they saw.

Something was obviously going on. It hadn't converted the whole town by any means; many didn't seem to know anything was happening. But many aspects of the community life had been touched, enough so that real estate people, for instance, knew where to point their clients who voiced interest in a "deep," or "charismatic," or "lively" Christian church. The schools felt it; so did the social agencies. Something was happening "up there on the ridge." A lot said it was good; some thought it might be a little weird, a nuisance. "There are always so many cars around the place," some said. "It's a real traffic problem."

But there it was, a nice, little Episcopal church—St. Paul's, Darien.

More Than a Building

The pretty little building labeled St. Paul's Episcopal Church obviously does not tell much of the story. In the first place, the congregation does not hold its Sunday services there, except for the early morning Communion service. It tried, by adding services to accommodate the growth, but when the number reached four, and some people weren't getting home from church until mid-afternoon, something had to be done.

The upshot was to move to the high school so everyone could worship together, four hundred fifty to six hundred each week and more than a thousand on special days. At the same time, the church building houses the children's church, with one hundred fifty or more attending.

But it doesn't stop there. On Sunday night, St. Paul's uses an Episcopal church in Stamford and fills it with four hundred or more people—including many young adults—in a freewheeling, prayer-and-praise type of meeting.

All of this, including the early risers at the eight A.M. Communion service, puts the Sunday attendance at twelve hundred or more.

And then, with Sunday out of the way, things start to get busy. A visitor can hardly keep up with it. On Tuesday morning, two hundred fifty people—mostly women—jam the sanctuary for worship, teaching, sharing, and Communion. It's the highlight of the week for many, large numbers of whom come from churches in the surrounding area.

On Wednesday nights, two to three hundred people pack the parish hall for forty-five minutes of singing and ninety minutes of Bible lecture. Again, many are from neighboring churches.

The young people take over on Friday nights, with everything from communal meals to Bible studies to service projects.

And those are only the formal activities. I found it impossible to check out the smaller meetings and less publicized events. "Bible studies in homes have been popping up faster than crabgrass, from Westchester to Westport," one writer said. The telephone prayer chains and partnerships seemed to go on and on. And the so-called "extended families," designed to meet parishioners' needs for more intimate fellowship, involved seven hundred people meeting anywhere from once a week to once a month.

The icing on the cake comes with Parish Renewal Weekends when hundreds from all parts of the country come for three days of immersion in St. Paul's life.

I finally gave up trying to count the number of people involved. It was too complicated. First, there was overlapping; then the irregular involvement of people from other places; then the low-profile, virtually unknown activities, like personal counseling, among lay people.

But if I couldn't handle quantity, how about quality? What was happening to the people?

—Ed Leaton's was a moving story. He was the current senior warden—sort of the official head layman in an Episcopal church—who some time ago lost two of his children in their early teens to muscular dystrophy. Like other victims of the dread disease, the two young boys went through the horrible cycle of first finding that they could no longer run. Then they couldn't walk. And after a while, standing or even sitting were too much.

"I committed my life to Jesus, and felt perfect peace in the eye of the storm," the business executive said. "It really is the 'peace that passes all understanding.' "

He made it through. The death of each boy was transformed from a tragedy into a victorious event. In particular did the case of one, Ken, touch all who knew him; people were inevitably drawn closer to God as they saw the faith of the boy.

Toward the end, Ken himself said, "I can see that an awful lot of people would never have known about Jesus if it weren't for me."

—Helen Mahon was the food services director at St. Paul's, heading a team of forty women who volunteered their time to prepare hot lunches every day at the church for all present and to work wonders with food at special events, like dinners to welcome new members.

"It's the Holy Spirit who gives me the joy I have in doing all I do and the strength to do it," she said smiling. "I don't get tired like I used to, though I'm doing twice as much as ever. And I don't get headaches any more."

—Martyn Minns, a former Mobil Oil executive, had just completed three years at seminary, followed by ordination. He and his wife, Angela, both British, had wrestled weeks and months over how to cope with what they perceived to be a call to the ministry for Martyn.

"We just don't see at all how it's going to work out, but I'm sure it will," she said at the time.

The final door was opened when St. Paul's parishioners took it upon themselves to meet expenses for them and their four children—$15,000 a year—to permit Martyn to attend three years of seminary in Virginia. His graduation and return, to the ministerial staff, was finally accomplished.

—Sally Sprague was an outgoing young housewife who, by then, laughed easily. "St. Paul's saved our marriage," she said. "We weren't terribly compatible. My husband was a workaholic. We were concerned about social status and had joined a country club which we couldn't afford. Our values have changed. We spend more time with the children. Our money goes further, and we spend it more for the Lord."

She smiled broadly, and then continued: "I had a case of

glaucoma, which disappeared after prayer. The doctor said, 'I don't understand it, but you're healed.' "

—Gordon Lyle was still a stockbroker. But he gave up several days a week to teach a Bible study at the Darien YMCA, to provide personal counseling along with his wife, Connie, and to give extraordinary leadership to a wide range of Christian activities. Together, he and his wife had helped dozens to find new meaning in life.

—One executive, who asked to remain anonymous, found faith in Christ and then had it sorely tested. He lost his job. And he couldn't find another one; placement of a highly qualified businessman does not always come easy. Finally, he needed help, and the Darien church was there, providing money for food and mortgage payments.

The man described the ordeal in the simplest terms: "I am a reborn and committed Christian. My old self has been left behind. I am striving in all aspects of my life to do what Christ would want me to do, at home and in my work. While the Lord has tested me, He has always helped me. Help always came before I reached the breaking point."

—Another much younger man who once sold a thousand dollars worth of cocaine a week was so thoroughly healed that he ended up working full time to take the good news of Christ to high school students, subsequently marrying and heading to college to finish his education.

—Lee Buck, a senior vice president of the New York Life Insurance Company, had emerged as one of the country's outstanding lay evangelists and banquet speakers. He described some of the background to that emergence: "My primary thrust was to be successful in business. We have moved twenty-three times in twenty-one years. I went to church because that's what successful people do. It was sort of expected. I never expected any answers to my prayers. But when I finally reached the top, I still did not feel fulfillment or peace. "Then the Lord worked a little miracle," he recalled.

Buck unreservedly embraced Jesus Christ as Lord of his life and that life has never been the same. Less well known than his rise as a public witness for Christ was the work he and his wife, Audrey, did in their home. With four children of their own, they began taking in foster children. At last count they had opened their home and life to seven, each being helped to overcome emotional problems ranging from drug abuse to suicide attempts.

Yes, in the Darien church there was a distinct quality. The list of those delivered from smashed, seemingly ruined lives was endless. Women whose eyes once revealed only desperate hollowness had been restored to whole life in their families. Men whose eyes had burned only with the fires of ambition and lust had been made fit for their lives as husbands and fathers. Men, women, and children whose emotions had been shattered, seemingly beyond healing safety, were reaching out to serve others.

Mike McManus is one of those men who is genuinely comfortable with statistics and other forms of data, trends, and interpretation of facts. He provided a significant view of the activity at St. Paul's placed against a backdrop of national and international indicators.

"There are signs of death in national church statistics," he said flatly, "those gathered each year by the National Council of Churches. For example, since 1966, there has been a 15 to 20 per cent shrinkage of church membership in most mainline denominations—among American Baptists, Episcopalians, Lutherans, Methodists, Presbyterians, and the United Church of Christ. In the Episcopal church alone, which really provides a good contrast with St. Paul's, the loss has been 600,000 members during that time, more than a thousand a week."

I looked at the figures for St. Paul's. He was right. The contrast was devastating. In the first five years with Fullam as rector, Sunday attendance at the Darien church climbed from 250 to 1,200. It might be the most heavily attended Episcopal church in the United States, week in and week out, with all of its activities tabulated.

Completing my revisit, I turned the car back onto Mansfield Avenue and drove away from town. Spotting a promising, country looking road, I turned onto it and drove through the quiet, fading afternoon. Occasionally I detected a house set back in the woods, with a long, winding driveway leading to it. But mostly I was aware of just the beauty of the Connecticut countryside, the soft brownness, the richness of old New England.

Images of St. Paul's church and its gentle people flitted in and out of my mind. Can this be? Can anything good come out of Darien? It was more than numbers. The lame walk, the deaf hear, the poor have good news preached to them, the poor rich—

How did this come about?

CHAPTER THREE

Early Days

It was 1940. Everett was ten.

"It's irreversible," Dr. Bertrand said to Rex and Mary Fullam. "He's going to lose his eyesight."

It was as blunt as that.

The Fullams had been taking their youngest child to the eye doctor for nearly a year, almost daily it seemed at times. They recalled vividly the day Dr. Bertrand in Montpelier had said, after interminable examination, "I think I know what he has; it's very rare. And I would like consultation with the doctors in Hanover."

The boy wasn't gradually losing his eyesight or anything like that, although it never was strong. He was afflicted with a sort of short circuiting of the link between his brain and the optic nerves. When the short circuit occurred, he was totally blind, and this was occurring with increasing frequency. One day it would be final.

The trips to the Dartmouth clinic in Hanover were unending, but the findings were the same. The condition was irreversible.

One day the doctors counseled Mr. and Mrs. Fullam about the future. "We recommend that you get as much information as possible into the boy's brain. Let him see and learn as much as possible so he can draw on it in the future."

They made a number of practical suggestions, such as teaching him to use a typewriter and taking him on a trip around the country to see as much of it as possible. Mr. Fullam, a lightning protection specialist whose business took him on the road a lot, had wanted to go to Texas soon. So it was agreed: Everett and his parents would combine a trip covering about half of the United States with a visit to Texas.

They set out in January, deep winter in their home state of Vermont, and soaked up the beauty, the wonder, the strangeness, the rarities, the commonplaces of their huge native land. Not every day was a good one for Everett, however. The blindness hit unexpectedly and often. His parents wondered whether he would last out the trip, but they determined to travel as much as possible only on those days when he could see.

It was a fabulous trip for the ten-year-old. He would not forget it or its lessons.

They were on their last leg north on his birthday, July 1, and they stopped at the wondrous Mammoth Cave National Park in central Kentucky. The myriad of avenues and domes, rivers and lakes, beautiful archways and other formations was dazzling.

Jammed full of visions and memories, the three arrived in Lowell, Massachusetts, on a Wednesday night to visit Everett's older sister, Virginia. They were almost home.

It was midweek meeting night at the Nazarene church Virginia attended, and they all went to the service. It was a good meeting, with nothing out of the ordinary until Margaret Stewart began to pray for Everett. A missionary returned from India, she really didn't know much about him, only that he had some quite serious eye problem, and she prayed a rather simple prayer for his healing during the rather simple service.

Thirty-eight years later, Terry Fullam said, "I've never had that eye problem since that moment."

Now, Terry has always spoken with great admiration and respect for his early Christian upbringing. He often said, "The wisest decision I ever made was in the choice of my parents. They were godly people—godly people. They *knew* the Lord, and that was the most evident thing about them. The earliest memories I have are of the two highest people I knew on earth who were on their knees before one whom they regarded as higher than themselves.

"And yet," he explained with a kindly smile, "faith for healing was not a feature of my family's very lively Christian life."

But their son was healed, quite obviously by God, as a result of prayer. There was no escaping it. Even the doctors acknowledged that "something" had happened unquestionably, something quite unexpected. And they tested and they tested, but there was no additional explanation.

"We always tied it in with that incident," Terry said. "In my own mind I've always thought of it as a definite healing of the Lord."

But he refrained, even in later years, from speaking often about the healing, partly out of fear of misunderstanding about God's working in his life and partly to avoid any "can-you-top-this" mentality.

"It would be easy to overemphasize this as the deciding factor in my life," he said. "In fact, I've had people who did hear about it come up and say to me, 'Well, I'd sure find it a lot easier to believe in God if I'd had something like that happen to me.'

"And while that's true in some people's lives, it just wasn't the case in mine. I believe I would have been the same way had I ended up blind. You see, for me, the Word—the teaching of the Word—was the deciding factor."

Yet, even in that moment, he marveled, quietly, rather boyishly, at God's tremendous grace.

A Mother's Influence

It may have been a matter of genes; it may have been the amount of exposure. But, whatever, his mother was probably the most dominant influence on Terry's life. This is not to suggest lack of influence by Mr. Fullam, for his father was crucial to his upbringing, and happily so. But Rex's work caused him to travel much. Furthermore, although he was four years younger than his wife, he died during Terry's senior year in high school.

It seems certain that Mary Fullam the teacher was responsible for Terry Fullam the teacher.

"She's probably the best teacher I've ever known," he said many years later—this from a man whom scores describe as the best teacher they've ever known.

"She can teach anything she understands," Fullam declared. "It's an analytical ability, I guess—the ability to look at a complex matter, break it down into its component parts, explain them, and then put them back together, explaining why they go together."

He stopped a moment, then said matter-of-factly, with no trace of pride, "I guess that's what I'm able to do, and I guess I inherited it."

Mary went right into teaching after two years at Boston University, and one of her high school students was her future husband. She taught at all levels—grade school, high school, college—and handled most subjects, including English and Latin.

"She can explain English grammar, to anyone who really wants to learn, in only four hours," Terry said. "I've never seen anything like it. She just sees through things."

After her husband's death, she returned to teaching and finally went back to school herself, taking summer courses at Barrington College when her son was a professor there.

"I had her in class," Terry said, "and she's a good student. She's been a reader all her life and quite a scholar."

At the age of seventy-five, Mrs. Fullam received her bachelor's degree at Barrington. That day, *The Providence Journal* photographed her in cap and gown astride son Terry's motorcycle, one of the few things mechanical that falls into the category of "passion" with him. The picture subsequently was sent around the country by a wire service.

Probably the most telling effect on young Everett from this extraordinary talent of his mother came in early childhood as he insisted on attending the Bible class she taught in church. "I much preferred hers to the one I was supposed to attend," he said. It was there that the Scriptures unfolded and came alive to him.

Additionally, the Fullams considered it their solemn responsibility to train their children in the Scriptures in other ways. "We literally discussed the Scriptures when we sat down to eat, when we got up in the morning, when we went out, when we returned. They asked us questions, and we talked, and we listened. They didn't care much whether we understood it all or not. They said if we could only hide it in our hearts, it would give the Holy Spirit something to work on in later years."

In 1975, Mrs. Fullam, her eyes sparkling and the lines

of her New England matron's face furrowing quite beautifully somehow, told me of the hours and hours her young son would spend with the Bible day after day, even before he was ten years old. "I'd see the light shining from his room long after he was to have been asleep," she said, chuckling, "and I'd look in and he'd be poring over that worn King James Bible of his. He devoured it."

Fullam summed up his early years this way: "It's hard to describe my parents to you, because the only word I can think of to describe them is so old-fashioned that I even wonder if you'll know what it means. They were *godly*. And we were brought to know and to love the Lord Jesus Christ very early."

Those Pentecostals

The summer afternoon was beautiful, in Vermont's special way. The direct sun was hot but not relentless, and the breeze blew. Young Terry, who was still called Everett, was with his brother, Rex Jr., who was ten years older, a bit more adventuresome, and, more importantly, a licensed driver.

Somehow they fell to talking about a group of people in their small city whom they found terribly fascinating, as long as they were at arm's length. They were the people from the Pentecostal church.

Rex and Everett had heard all kinds of strange stories about them, especially about their summer camp meetings, which were going on right that moment fifteen or twenty miles from town.

"Now you have to understand," Fullam said many years later, shaking his head rather sadly, "that we had absolutely nothing to do with them. We did not go into their church, nor did they come into ours."

The Fullams were Baptists.

"Somehow," he continued, "we did not move in the

same ecclesiastical orbit, you see. Our young people did nothing with their young people. There really was no contact."

But there were rumors, and Everett listened to them avidly. Nothing very specific was ever said about those camp meetings, but the innuendoes were more than enough for lively imaginations and prejudices. It seemed obvious that something "weird" was going on.

So on that lazy afternoon, Everett and Rex Jr. took a ride.

"We drove out to the place," Fullam recollected, "and before we even got there you could hear them. I had never heard such noise in my life!"

They reached the gate and Rex stopped the car, looking at Everett. "Do you think we should go in?"

Without hesitation, the younger boy replied, "Yes, let's go in." His words far exceeded his courage.

They drove through the gate, turned the car around, and left it facing outward, "in case we had to make a quick getaway."

"Now you couldn't see the people from where you parked the car," Terry recounted, "because there was a little rise in the hill, and down on the other side was a sort of natural amphitheater. And so we got out of the car and made our way to the top of the hill and peered over. I couldn't believe my eyes. I had never seen anything like this in my entire life. Here were hundreds of people singing and shouting like you wouldn't believe. They were waving their hands in the air. I didn't know whether they were shaking hands with God or what. I had never seen anything like it."

Again shaking his head, he paused, and went ahead, "In our church we knelt and prayed very quietly. But these people were doing this in a most loud way. And I watched the whole thing with absolute amazement. And even though I was a child, I remember saying to myself, 'Can this possibly be of God?' And I concluded that it was not."

Again he paused a moment. "You see, I have to tell you that, because very early in my life I formed a strong prejudice against anything remotely associated with the word 'Pentecostal.' To me it was the lunatic fringe. By now I've learned something about myself and also about man, and God has forgiven me for my most uncharitable attitude, which I sustained for many years."

Prejudiced or not, young Fullam saw something crystallize in himself that afternoon: He liked things, both inside and outside the church, to be done "decently and in order."[1] To him, at that time, that meant quietly.

"The idea of such noise, singing, shouting, and dancing about seemed to my childish mind to be so absolutely inappropriate before the eyes of almighty God. I was quite serious, you see—mistaken, oh, yes, but very serious. And I formed a prejudice even as a child against anything termed 'Pentecostal.' "

God Speaks—Sometimes

Elementary and secondary education in Vermont public schools, interrupted by two years at a private Christian academy in Tennessee, left Everett Fullam successfully moving along the road to a music career. At eighteen, he was well experienced as a pianist and organist and was ready for even more study and work.

He had studied under an outstanding teacher, Katrina Munn from Bradford, Vermont, a Juilliard graduate, and her decision to move to a little town in western New York, Wellsville, left a hole in young Fullam's path. So he decided to go to Wellsville himself, sharing some of her overloaded teaching schedule, serving as organist in a church, and continuing his studies with her, preparatory to studying at the Eastman School of Music.

---

[1] 1 Corinthians 14:40

Several significant events in the preparation of Terry Fullam occurred in western New York. In the first place, he overworked himself, ending up with eighty students, the organist's job in two churches, the leadership in Youth for Christ locally, the necessity to practice six hours a day himself, and work on music-related subjects. But he was strong, and well on the way in the development of the stamina that would be required of him in later years

One morning in the winter of 1949 he was in his quite comfortable studio in the Methodist church. It had a fireplace and contained his two pianos—a grand and a spinet—and even had its own entrance. He read from the Bible and began to pray in preparation for the coming day of work. He was extremely busy and prospering unusually for his age, but he was giving much thought to what lay ahead for him. His teacher, Miss Munn, had overtaxed herself, become ill, and returned to Vermont. Was he in danger of doing the same thing? And what did God have in mind for his life?

As he prayed, he underwent a totally new experience. He actually *heard* the voice of the Lord. It wasn't audible; he was quite sure of that. But the result was the same. He heard within himself the words of God. They were distinct:

"I am calling you to nourish and beget the life of God in the souls of men."

And that was all. But his thoughts took over, and he immediately recalled instances in the Bible where people had declared, "The Lord said unto me—" and he then knew this was what they had meant.

But, even then, he was logician enough to see that something was out of order in what God had just said. "It should be beget and nourish," he thought. "You have to beget before you can nourish."

He quickly addressed this challenge to the Lord, and

just as distinctly as in the first case, he heard the words:
"It is not beget and nourish. What I've said, I've said."

The eighteen-year-old musician remained on his knees
and puzzled over the exchange. What could it mean?

It certainly sounded as though he was being called to
feed, somehow, to give or to teach maybe, in such a way
that people would be "born again." It still didn't seem
quite logical. One had to be born before he could be
nourished. "Nourish and beget." He said it aloud.

All he could do was put the experience on the shelf and
wait. But he never forgot it.

Close on the heels of this was another episode that
began when the pastor of the Methodist church housing
his studio handed Fullam a book. "I think you'd like this,"
he said.

Everett took it and examined the cover. It was titled
Deeper Experiences of Famous Christians, a book then
out of print but later reissued.

"Thanks," he replied, still studying the cover. "It looks
interesting."

Back in his room that night, Fullam, an insatiable
reader, dove into the book. It was a collection of stories
about people God had used to change the course of
history. And, intriguingly, they all told of an experience
with God, sometimes years after their initial conversion,
in which they found the power of Christ in their lives.
Some called that experience "entire sanctification," some
a "second blessing," and others a "baptism of love." There
were some who called it "the baptism of the Holy Spirit."

As he read those descriptions, his hair practically stood
on end; he realized they were all talking about the same
thing, a work of the Holy Spirit.

Days passed, and he read more. And he began to
examine himself in the light of the experiences of those
famous people. He knew, of course, that he was a

Christian. That was not the issue. He knew he belonged to the Lord—he had entered into eternal life—and he was even serving Him.

"But," he said nearly thirty years later, "there were a number of things in my life that I knew were out of harmony with the will of God. And the strange thing about it was that there didn't seem to be an awful lot I could do about it. I had often prayed about it; I had confessed many of these things. But nothing seemed to happen."

He thought carefully about it one night in his room in Wellsville. He had developed a profound hunger for a deeper touch of the Spirit of God on his life. He thought further. "It's amazing that the church has lasted this long if other people don't have more than I have." And he knew he wasn't alone in that conviction. "What is the problem? The Bible talks about a life that doesn't bear much resemblance to what I've experienced or what others I see have experienced."

He sat for several minutes, and everything was quiet. At last he blurted out, half-aloud, "Lord, tonight is the night! I've got to settle this thing once and for all."

So he locked the door, pulled down the window shades, and got down on his knees, Bible in hand. He was very direct in his approach: "Lord, I'm not going to rise from my knees until you give me whatever it is I need!"

Later he reflected on that moment. "Now notice, I didn't try to tell God what I needed. I supposed He ought to know. I said, 'Lord, whatever you want to do in my life, that's what I want.' And I began to review my whole life. I went back as far as I could go. I confessed every sin I could think of; I even made up a few. I took every earthly possession in this world I had—and you can be sure it wasn't much—and systematically I offered it to the Lord. I said, 'Lord, I will commit to you every day I shall live from this moment on, if you will give me what I need.' "

And in like manner he prayed through the night. Apparently nothing happened.

"Whatever it was I expected, somehow I did not receive it. Now I still don't know why I didn't. I know one thing: There was never a point in my life, before or since, when I was more yielded to the Lord, any more open to Him."

As dawn approached, he rose to his feet. "Well, maybe I'm not old enough," he said to himself, dead serious. "I'm certainly not good enough, if that's what it takes." He hesitated. "But I know that's not it; it has to be a matter of grace. I guess God just does not want to do anything."

He sat in a chair and was quiet for a few seconds. His boldness returned. "Now, Lord, remember this night. Don't forget it. I met you more than halfway. And I just want you to remember that. If you're not satisfied with my life, it's your fault."

It sounded more presumptuous than it probably was, for he was merely saying what he felt and was talking to someone from whom no secrets are hidden.

He looked at the book the pastor had given him, shook his head, and spoke conclusively to God: "Now Lord, I just simply can't think about this any more. It's been consuming too much of my time. I did what I could, and you didn't do what you should, and therefore I'm just not going to think about it any more."

A Turn in the Road

The weeks and months drifted by, and Fullam worked harder than ever, enrolling in the Eastman School on a part-time basis to work toward a degree and continuing his other activities.

Once again, a book played a major role in his life. This time it was a volume he picked up at the Wellsville Public

Library—a book of philosophy.

"I was hooked on the first page," he recalled. "I loved it."

He had felt an uneasiness, something like a tug within himself, suggesting his life and young career were too narrow. His lively mind felt a bit confined. Furthermore, he occasionally glanced at his mental shelf where the word from the Lord about "nourishing and begetting" lay quietly. He had begun to say things like "maybe there is something more."

The philosophy book, and the dozen others that quickly followed, turned the nagging sensation into a conviction, and then into a decision. After three years in western New York, he would take up the formal study of philosophy.

He enrolled as a freshman at Gordon College in Boston (which subsequently expanded to a campus in Wenham on the Massachusetts North Shore). Four years of straight A's were followed by graduate study at Harvard and Boston University where he completed all of the work for his doctorate except for his dissertation.

Fullam's music career did not end, however. It served him especially well in the summertime during these early years when he worked as a music director at Christian conferences in New Hampshire, resulting indirectly in several events affecting his life significantly.

One of the less profound events came just before he began his studies at Gordon. He was working at the New England Fellowship conference with a musician friend named Ted, and right away someone felt the duo of "Ted and Everett" didn't sound just right. "Ted and Terry" sounded better, so Everett L. Fullam from that summer on was more popularly known as Terry.

A more life-affecting event also resulted from Terry's work at the New Hampshire conference. A pastor from the state capital of Concord saw Terry there and invited him to be the music director at his church. He accepted. That meant he had to come from Boston every weekend and needed a place to stay for two nights. He was put up in the home of a family of Norwegian ancestry, the Andresens.

Two of the Andresen daughters sang in the church choir, and Fullam found their company increasingly and exceedingly pleasant, especially Ruth's. She was very pretty, strongly committed to Christ, thoughtful and keen of mind, yet disarmingly self-effacing. Their long walks and talks in the quietness of New Hampshire showed a rare balance between Terry's surging curiosity and garrulousness and Ruth's quiet wisdom and gentleness, a balance that held steady through months of testing.

Then, on September 27, 1952, just one year to the day after their first meeting, they were married in the little Concord church.

Fullam's busy schedule continued throughout his years of education in Boston. Before beginning his graduate work at Harvard, for example, he took on the music minister's job on a part-time basis at a well-known downtown Baptist church, Tremont Temple. He did this work either full time or part time over the next eight years, which were times of important molding in his life.

Two years into his graduate studies, he also took on part-time teaching jobs, mostly in philosophy—first at Calvin Coolidge College in Boston, then at Northeastern University in Boston, and finally at Barrington College near Providence, Rhode Island. He ultimately moved to

Rhode Island to teach full time at Barrington and part time at the Providence campus of the University of Rhode Island.

A teaching career was well launched.

A Season of Discontent

Fullam's spiritual development was notable during the Boston years, beginning with his arrival at Gordon College, a Christian liberal arts institution. His roots were deep and solid, set pretty much in the Baptist tradition, although not formally or exclusively so. He had not enrolled in any particular fellowship.

By the time he arrived for his freshman year—having been on his own for three years—the pangs of discontent with what he was seeing in the church generally were being felt. He had confronted God in Wellsville with his dissatisfaction over his own experience, and he was moving toward the same kind of dissatisfaction with church life as he had seen it thus far.

"There were just so many things about it which did not appeal to me," he said twenty-six years later over breakfast in a little Darien restaurant.

"When I was at Gordon," he continued, "I used to get up very early in the morning and study, and then I would leave the house about five-thirty every morning and go for a long walk. I did this for four years, really."

He paused, and I could almost see those days passing across his mind. Finally he continued: "And early on, I found this little church called St. Clement's down on Mass. Avenue." Like all Bostonians, he said it just that way—Mass. Avenue, never Massachusetts Avenue. "It was near Symphony Hall. And it was Roman Catholic; St. Clement's Eucharistic Shrine, it was called. And I knew all the Protestant reasons, all the things where I disagreed with the Catholics, but there was something about that church that drew me in there."

Again he stopped momentarily before continuing haltingly as he tried to recall the magnetism, the compelling moments of those days. "It was a church of perpetual adoration—There were nuns—in white habits—that were in there venerating the sacrament—twenty-four hours a day. And there was something about, you know, about going into that place.

"At precisely six o'clock in the morning the organ began to play—always—and there was never a word spoken. They didn't have any services—but here there were people worshiping God other than in a service of some sort—and I was strongly drawn to that place."

The mystery of being *drawn* there—repeated several times during those few minutes—was obviously significant to him. It hadn't merely *happened*, in his view.

"I went there for four years almost," he said, pressing ahead with his recollections. "And I'd go and just pray —and read—It was a beautiful building—you know—It was quiet—this soft organ music in the background. And it just opened in me a real hunger for something or other—other than the rather frenetic, hard-sell evangelism that I had been accustomed to, where it seemed to me that often there was no worship at all. Everything had become evangelism. They would give an invitation at the end of every service—and it didn't matter whether it was appropriate or not, whether the Spirit was moving in that way or not—it was expected. Many times, of course, nobody would come forward—most of the time, in fact, nobody would come.

"And this was so different—this worship at that little church."

Over the years, those pangs of discontent worsened. Everything he was seeing persuaded him that something was fundamentally wrong. There was strife and division on every side, despite a rugged devotion to the preaching of the gospel and to an evangelistic heritage.

"It seemed to me," he said that morning over breakfast, "that it was just a terrible, terrible parody of what you find in the New Testament. It just utterly turned me off."

He sipped from his milk. "And that drove me back to the Bible," he continued. "For the first time in my life I began to look at the whole business of what a church is—you know. And the more I studied, the more convinced I was that much of what I had been brought up to believe was just not true at all."

Heavy lines of sadness darkened his face as he looked past me, unseeing. He was a man lacking in over-critical spirit and the memory of those discoveries so long ago obviously distressed him.

"I was convinced that the kind of radical independence that is so much a part of the mentality of the church I was seeing was not right. They had carried it to the point where they had no concept—zero concept—of the church as the body of Christ, none whatever. They had a concept of salvation, but that was a one-to-one relationship with God and had no dimensions horizontally at all—and no real notion of the Holy Spirit, nothing like this."

His face brightened gradually as he talked his way through that long-ago revelation. "I began to see that what I thought to be the gospel actually was only a truncated version of it, only a little portion of it."

Terry and Ruth had been in Providence about forty-eight hours when the telephone rang with a call from a man named Stewart. It was Alexander Stewart, then rector of St. Mark's Episcopal Church in Riverside and later bishop of western Massachusetts.

A friendly, fast-talking man with a bright sense of

humor, he went boldly to the point with Terry. "I'd like to talk to you about becoming the organist at our church," he said.

Terry was startled. "How did you know about me?" he asked with equal bluntness.

It turned out that a Barrington colleague familiar with his work at Tremont Temple and other churches in New England had told Stewart, "This is the guy you should get. He's coming from a big church in Boston."

"Well," Terry said, swallowing the last of his milk that morning in Darien, "I was ready for a change. I had never attended an Episcopal service anywhere in my life, but I was ready for a change; I knew that.

"So I went, and I think I knew from the first service on—I just knew I had come home. There were things about it I didn't quite understand, and I didn't at that time know the history of it so much, and it seemed kind of Catholic to me, but that appealed to me because of my experience at St. Clement's Eucharistic Shrine for four years.

"And the Eucharist!" He broke into a wide smile. "I discovered the Eucharist. I couldn't get enough of it. I looked around—I was like a person who had been without something in his diet—and I began to look around and found a church, St. Stephen's in Providence, that had a daily Eucharist. And for years I went almost every day of the week—up at seven o'clock and drive into Providence. I just couldn't get enough of it!

"That opened a whole new world for me, and I knew that I had found my family in the faith."

A Man Named Bennett

Fullam soon became an invaluable aide to Father Stewart at St. Mark's Church, spreading out from his work as organist and choirmaster to teaching Bible studies and helping in other activities. He and the rector became increasingly close friends.

So it was not surprising one day in 1961 when Stewart called and asked Terry to fill in for him at a meeting that night and bring the guest speaker to the rectory to spend the night. "I've run into this conflict and my wife and I can't go. Will you and Ruth go and after the meeting bring him back here?"

Terry waited a second and then spoke into the telephone, "Who's the man?"

"He's Dennis Bennett from St. Mark's in Van Nuys, California."

Terry paused again. He knew about Father Dennis Bennett and that church—a regular St. Minks and All Sables—a place where one might go for the smell of perfume but never the odor of sanctity. He had only recently read in *Time* and *Newsweek* magazines about the "strange things" taking place in that most unlikely environment.

"I'd love to go," he said to Stewart.

Bennett had been at the center of controversy over a "new" phenomenon that seemed to be occurring in various parts of the mainline churches. It was called the baptism in the Holy Spirit.

"I've never seen anybody filled with the Holy Spirit," Fullam thought. He wasn't sure if their faces would be shining or their eyes spewing fire or their hair standing on end, or what. His only experience of that sort had come from a distance at that Pentecostal camp in Vermont many, many years ago.

Terry and Ruth arrived at the Old Colony Motor Hotel on Narragansett Boulevard and found themselves among two hundred seventy people, mostly clergymen, awaiting the arrival of the guest speaker. Finally, Dennis Bennett walked through the door of the big meeting room, and Fullam's heart sank.

"It absolutely sank to the floor," Terry recalled. "Now you have to understand he's really not a bad-looking man. Some people might even think him handsome. But, you see, he had a crew cut—and somehow my image of a Spirit-filled man did not include a crew cut. Now I don't get all bothered about the length of a person's hair, but at that time it just didn't fit in with my mental image of what a Spirit-filled person ought to look like."

Terry wasn't really sure what he had expected—perhaps something like the popular representations of John the Baptist or maybe St. Peter; he wasn't sure.

The meeting began and Bennett was called upon to speak. "He didn't preach," Fullam recalled, "he just talked—for an hour and twenty minutes!"

Dennis told in some detail what had happened to him and to his church—how first one couple had come into a new experience with Jesus through the Holy Spirit, with their lives changing drastically for the better, and then how he had been so deeply impressed that he went to see them. He, too, underwent that "new experience"—the baptism in the Holy Spirit—and his ministry was revolutionized, also for the better. The Lord had become real and personal to him, and he had begun to minister in power and love that he hadn't known before.

Terry squirmed in his seat. He had a hundred questions to ask. "Just wait till I get him alone in the car," he thought.

Finally Bennett concluded his talk and said, "Now if there's anybody here who wants to be baptized in the Holy Spirit, we've secured a suite of rooms on the second floor, and we would invite you to come up."

Then he said something comforting to Terry. "If you've

already received the baptism in the Holy Spirit, don't come to the rooms; you'll frighten everyone away. We will receive the Holy Spirit tonight in the Episcopal way."

He smiled handsomely, and Fullam breathed easier. He assumed that meant "decently and in order." If he had to go through with this thing, that was the only way he could do it.

The instant Bennett dismissed the general meeting, a couple Terry and Ruth had not seen for a year or more charged up to them. The man was a violinist with the Boston Symphony Orchestra—he was on Terry's wave length musically—and both he and his wife were professing Christians.

The wife blurted out, "Do you know what has happened to us?"

The Fullams didn't, so they shook their heads.

"Well, since we've seen you—in the last year we have all been baptized in the Holy Spirit, the children and us, too." •

Terry just stared.

"And what a tremendous difference it has made in our lives," the man said. "It has changed everything."

Terry continued to stare. Ruth sort of half-smiled, looked up at Terry, and then back at the couple.

And then the woman looked him straight in the eye and rather dramatically—embarrassingly so to Terry—asked, "Have you been baptized in the Holy Spirit?"

Terry replied slowly, "No," thinking to himself: "Dear lady, I could give you a lecture on the Holy Spirit; I could take you on a week's Bible study of the subject."

But he answered her question, knowing she meant it in the sense Dennis Bennett had described.

The woman smiled. "I think you will very soon."

"Well," Fullam said rather tepidly, "I'm willing." But

his mind raced back to the time in Wellsville many years earlier when he had spent the whole night asking the Lord for something like what she and Bennett were talking about. "He didn't do anything for me then," he thought, "and I don't see that there's anything different now."

The exchange with the violinist and his wife delayed Terry and Ruth in getting to the rooms on the second floor and they were the last of about thirty-five people to arrive. Bennett was talking.

"Now," he said, "I'm going to lay hands on you and pray for you. But you must understand that when I lay hands on you the spiritual power isn't dripping out of my shoulders and going into yours. I only lay hands upon you simply following the example of the apostles. Jesus is the baptizer in the Holy Spirit. I'm not."

He stopped a moment, that bright, handsome smile covering his face. "What I want you to do after I pray for you is turn your whole heart to the Lord and begin to pray to Him—but not in English."

Many years later, Fullam told of that moment:

"You cannot describe the feeling that came over me at that moment. You see, in his talk he had mentioned speaking in tongues and that was, to me, like swinging on a chandelier. Remember, I had spent years and years studying abnormal psychology, and I wasn't the least bit interested in speaking in tongues. I could imagine myself standing up on the organ bench at St. Mark's Church speaking in tongues. Why, they'd throw me out of the place! And they ought to!"

So Fullam built up his courage at that moment in the hotel room and raised his hand. Bennett nodded kindly toward him.

"Father Bennett, I'm very interested in what you're calling the baptism of the Holy Spirit, but frankly I'm just not much interested in this tongues business."

Bennett smiled again, very benignly, and said simply, "Well, many times it comes with the package."

Fullam only stared—unsmiling. "Somehow," he said later, "I felt I was not called upon to instruct him at that point."

Bennett began to pray, starting with the person on his right. Terry knew the man. He was the pastor of a large Lutheran church in Providence. He knew him to be well educated, a man with a respectable ministry—seemingly a balanced man. And Bennett prayed very quietly, "Lord Jesus, baptize this, your servant, in the Holy Spirit."

Fullam was stunned. The man began to pray in what sounded like a fully articulate, but unrecognizable, language. Terry strained to listen.

Bennett moved on to the next person, prayed for him, and the same thing happened. Then the next one. "It's like dominoes," Terry thought.

Terry and Ruth were kneeling just inside the door of the second room, and Bennett was getting closer. Terry was actually frightened. He prayed quickly, "Lord, I'm not here for some weird experience—especially that tongues business—but if there is something you have that can help me love you more perfectly and serve you more effectively, then I would like it."

Actually, Terry was afraid that nothing would happen. "I couldn't believe that anything would happen," he recalled. "Why should it? It hadn't years before, and I couldn't see why anything was different this time."

His recollection of the next few minutes was very vivid:

Well, when he got to us he stopped. We were kneeling at the corner of a bed. He stepped right by me, walked right by me, and started in on the other side of the room. So, you see, I know the feeling of a convict with a last-minute reprieve from the electric chair; I felt I had a little while left.

Finally he closed in from the other side and prayed for my wife first. That seemed ordinary enough; I couldn't tell that anything had happened, although she actually had received the baptism in the Spirit.

Then he got to me and he said, "Lord Jesus, baptize this, your very fearful servant, in the Holy Spirit."

That's all he said, and I didn't see any tongues of fire or hear any rushing, mighty wind, or feel any warmth or warm, slushy feeling in my heart. I wouldn't know a thing had happened—but then he said to me, "Turn your heart to the Lord and praise Him, but not in English."

And that was the closest I have ever come to a cardiac arrest. It was not only something I did not really want; I could not see any useful purpose for it—at least not for an Anglican. It seemed indecent to me. The only memory I had ever had was that very strange experience I had as a child with those very funny people while they were dancing about, working themselves into a frenzy and shooting themselves into orbit. And that was about the last thing I wanted to have happen to me, you can be sure. The whole thing could have aborted right there and then. Because it seemed to me—you see, I had spent years and years studying how to think, and then how to speak what I was thinking so that it would come out right—and it sounded like Father Bennett was saying, "What I really want you to do is put your brain in neutral, your tongue in high gear, and step on the gas."

And that was the hardest thing I have ever done in my life. But God gave me grace, and somehow I took a deep breath, felt like a fool, and started in.

To my complete astonishment, there it was—absolutely effortless! It just poured from me!

My dear wife, kneeling next to me, looked over and just wondered.

Well, that was now about thirteen years ago. I can tell you that that moment opened up a dimension of the life in Christ that I had not known before—a dimension of power for ministry and service. I wouldn't want you to think all problems were solved, or that instant maturity was reached, or anything like that, but there certainly was a connection with the power of the gospel at that moment that I had not known before and that has never left.

It has absolutely changed my life—and for it I profoundly thank our God.

Ordination

It was 1963. Fullam was taking the Barrington choir on tour, and the sense welled up within him as they traveled that he should seek ordination to the Episcopal priesthood. The preceding year, he had felt the same thing about joining the Episcopal church, and that had been accomplished.

He wasn't precisely sure why he thought it would be good to be ordained. He didn't feel called to the parish ministry, and he truly didn't see how ordination would change much. He already had a ministry; his Bible class at St. Mark's was flourishing with amazing results, and he was the organist and choirmaster. Why seek ordination? He wasn't sure, but the sense that he should would not go away.

So he wrote to Ruth, describing his feelings. Before mailing the letter he prayed, "Lord, if this is your will, cause us to agree on it."

Ruth wrote back quickly, "I think it would be

wonderful."

After his return, he went to see Bishop John Higgins of the Diocese of Rhode Island, who was positively impressed and sent him to see John Coburn, dean of the Episcopal Theological Seminary in Cambridge, Massachusetts, who is now Bishop of the Diocese of Massachusetts.

Coburn was impressed with Terry's academic record and his credentials as a college teacher. He said Fullam could probably be ordained with only one year full time at an Episcopal seminary and sent him back to Bishop Higgins with that recommendation. This posed a problem for Terry, because he was already committed to full-time teaching at Barrington the following year.

But he followed through, sharing his concerns with the bishop. It happened that that very day, the bishop had on his desk the canonical examinations to be given to four seminarians the next day in preparation for ordination. He also had before him copies of the previous year's exams and, during the course of their visit, asked Terry some questions from them. He readily answered them.

The bishop thought for a moment and said, "Why don't you come back tomorrow and sit in on the exams? It might be interesting."

The next day, Fullam took two of three tests that the seminarians were taking—on Scripture and on Greek. The theology test was to be given the following day.

The Scripture test was objective for the most part, with hundreds of questions, followed by a few essay questions and then an oral examination. The Greek test was routine. Fullam was confident he had done well on everything.

He arrived on the second day and the place was abuzz. Something was up. The examiners took him aside and spoke to him incredulously. He had attained a perfect score on the Scripture test, answering every one of the hundreds of questions correctly. Nothing like that had been done before. As for the oral exam, one said, "You should be giving the tests, not taking them."

Furthermore, the Greek results were excellent, and he went on to do well in theology.

He then met with Bishop Higgins, who said, "I don't think you need a year in seminary. You can go ahead and study on your own for those areas where you have had no training."

And that's what he did. Over the next three years, he studied liturgics, church history, moral theology, and Christian ethics by himself and passed the remaining canonical exams with ease.

In 1966 he was ordained a deacon, and in 1967 a priest, all without having spent one day in seminary, continuing as professor of biblical studies, philosophy, and logic at Barrington.

Taking on increased part-time duties at St. Mark's Church with his good friend, Alex Stewart, Fullam settled into his self-described "ivory tower life" in Rhode Island with never a thought toward any other kind of life. It seemed perfect.

Then came a late spring day—a Thursday—in 1972. Fullam had a heavy cold and was coughing badly, but he refused to yield to it, maintaining his full schedule and even adding to it. He was expected in Albany, New York, for a teaching mission the next day.

That night he was asked to serve as host to a Dutch evangelist who was to speak at a student meeting. He was Franz Schadee, who among other things had spent a lot of time taking Bibles behind the Iron Curtain.

After the public meeting, Terry took Schadee to a smaller room for a time of prayer and ministry with those desiring it. As they gathered, Terry's cough was more and more persistent, and he asked the people to pray for him, that he might be able to carry out the mission the following day.

They prayed, some laying hands on him, and as they concluded, Schadee, a tall, slender, dark-haired man, who had been standing across the room, approached Terry and began to speak prophetically. The room became very quiet, except for his heavily accented voice: "I, the Lord, am about to change the direction of your life. You are to enter a new ministry. I have prepared you for years. You are to go confidently."

As Terry listened, he didn't know what to make of the words. But he listened reverently and in faith. He knew that the Lord still spoke through His people.

The following week, Reg Jones called from Darien. During the call, as he found himself unable to say no flatly, the memory of Schadee's prophecy kept playing on the edge of his consciousness even though he couldn't focus perfectly on it.

Something was definitely going to happen.

CHAPTER FOUR

A Hard Question

While the Pharisees were gathered together,
Jesus asked them, Saying, What think ye of Christ?
whose son is he?[1]

It was Sunday, the first day of October, 1972, a year of
politics, intrigue, and conspiracy that was to leave an ugly
scar on the government of the United States. George
McGovern was challenging Richard Nixon for the
presidency. And reports arising from a bizarre break-in at
Democratic National Headquarters in a place called
Watergate flitted confusingly in and out of the
newspapers. But in Darien, Connecticut, the fall season
was magnificent.

A hush fell over the one hundred seventy-five people in
the little Episcopal church on Mansfield Avenue as they in
unison fixed their eyes on the dark brown, raised pulpit to
the left of the altar. A large man stood in it—Father
Everett L. Fullam, the new rector, a college professor.
Some of the people had seen him before, but quite a few
had not. The long black cassock and loose white surplice,
topped by the slender green stole signifying the season of
Trinity, made him seem even larger than he was.

[1]Matthew 22:41-42, KJV.

Phil March, an advertising man, studied Fullam. "You've got to give him credit for one thing," he thought grudgingly. "He's a heck of an imposing figure."

That very thought clicked into place in many minds. Some even resented it. "He looks pretty arrogant to me," said one middle-aged, slightly graying woman to herself.

The silence was heavy—no coughs, no shuffling of feet. Several mouths opened slightly, expectantly.

Fullam's customary smile was gone as his eyes moved quickly across the nearly filled sanctuary. He had finished the announcements, one about a junior choir rehearsal. The sun slanted sharply through the floor-to-ceiling window at the rear, casting shadows across the body of intent people.

"This morning, as I start my ministry among you"—his voice was sharp and clear, a trifle high—"I must ask your prayers."

A humble beginning, thought several.

"For I come in the assurance that this is the Lord's call as well as your own."

Humph. You could almost hear it in the pews.

"It is certainly my prayer that God will, in our time together, mold us and make us according to His will."

Several of the upturned faces smiled; others waited. Fullam continued, his apparent confidence unwavering:

"This past summer, as I spent a good deal of time alone, and thinking about this contemplated move, I felt the Lord speaking to me through the ancient words of the prophet Jeremiah. Jeremiah, speaking for the Lord, complained about the priests in his area. He said, 'The trouble with these people is that they do not speak the words of the Lord. They speak from their own minds.' "[2]

Several in the audience frowned. Was he going to start criticizing Arthur Lane?

The paraphrase of the prophet went on: " 'They speak

---

[2]Jeremiah 23:16.

with their own minds of thoughts and visions that they themselves have kindled.' Then, quoting the Lord, Jeremiah adds, 'If My priests would stand in My council and if they would listen to My word, they would hear it. And they would speak in a way that would enable My people to hear My voice.' "[3]

Fullam smiled broadly for the first time and looked into several faces halfway back in the crowd. Speaking of himself, he went on: "And then the Lord said to me, 'Will you be this kind of priest, one who will listen to My voice, that you might speak My word?' "

He paused for a second, as though to allow his listeners to insert his unspoken answer to the Lord, "Yes, I will be that kind of priest (despite the fact that I've never really tried it on a full-time basis before)."

His voice a shade lower now, he continued. "There are a great many things that are important to be heard these days about which you will not hear me speak. I will not be giving you opinions here. I will not be commenting on the news or on trends or any of that except as they pertain to the Word of God or it pertains to them. But it certainly is my prayer that I will be speaking the mind of the Lord. It is up to me to listen—to be in tune to His Holy Spirit. And I need your prayers with this—"

Phil March's thoughts broke into the conclusion of the sentence: "Man, you sure do." He was quite sure the thought was sympathetic, not hostile.

Fullam's opening remarks wound down quickly and he set off in another direction, raising himself to his full height and taking a quick glance at his wristwatch. His speaking tempo seemed to increase ever so slightly.

"I hope there is no one here this morning who has not given some thought to Jesus Christ."

---

[3]Jeremiah 23:22.

He went straight at them with several fast sentences about reading *of* Christ and hearing *of* Him, and then he set the theme of his sermon. "But yet almost two thousand years have passed since He walked among us on this earth, and there still comes to people of this generation—who find themselves in a Christian church on a Sunday morning—the very same question that our Lord put to the religious people of His own day, a question which has reverberated down through the corners of time, and which we must answer this morning. And that is: 'What think ye of Christ?' "

Silence filled the pause. And Terry, never speaking from notes or text, seemed to keep his eyes on every pew simultaneously. His rather stern look eased into a slight smile.

"Now I don't know why that should not be a perfectly proper question for one man to put to another. If I were to ask you what you think of President Nixon, or Senator George McGovern, I daresay most of you would have an opinion. And some of you would be quite willing to express it."

He almost chuckled. "Now, if this is true, why should we not expect people to make up their minds about Jesus Christ?

"I personally think it would be a great day in the church of Jesus Christ if people would just stand up and be counted," he added. "And I'm also convinced that what you and I think of President Nixon and Senator George McGovern will not matter much in a hundred years. Most of the men who sit in parliament and deliberate, most of the people whose names loom so large in today's newspapers, will all be forgotten in a hundred years."

Was he going to get anti-intellectual right there in such an intellectual, such an aware setting? There was a hint of squirming.

"But listen"—it was sharp enough to snap a few heads—"if Jesus Christ is who He said He was, if He is what our church and its creeds proclaim Him to be, then this is the supreme question of all of life."

He hesitated ever so slightly, and his right hand came up in front of him, chest high. He was almost pointing. "If it be true, if it be true that He is God in human form, if it be true that it was for us men and for our salvation that He came down from heaven and was implanted by the Holy Ghost in the Virgin Mary and became man,[4] surely this is the most important question we can possibly ask."

Reg Jones, a bass, was sitting with the choir. He looked down between his legs at the floor; his head nodded almost imperceptibly. Betty March, Phil's wife, two-thirds of the way back in the sanctuary, couldn't suppress a smile. Many faces didn't move.

But Fullam didn't let up. He knew his crowd. They had heard the gospel from Arthur Lane and others. But he had to establish his ground.

"Now I want to be perfectly clear on what it is I'm asking," he said, slowing his speech pattern considerably and leaning forward in the pulpit, creating a respectable air of intimacy. "I'm really *not* asking you this morning what you think about the Episcopal church, or the Presbyterians, or the Methodists, or the Baptists, or the Roman Catholics. I'm *not* asking you what you think about this priest or that priest or minister, or about this teaching or that. But I do want to ask you what you think about Jesus Christ."

He paused half a second. "In the Gospel that was read a few moments ago, we hear of Jesus turning to a crowd of Pharisees standing nearby and asking them this question: 'What think ye of Christ? Whose son is he?' And that's the question I'd like to ask you."

Terry was remarkably composed. He was in control.

---

[4] Nicene Creed.

There was no indication of nervousness simply because he was not nervous. He was a teacher, and he was teaching.

Later, JoAnn Irvine, the parish secretary and subsequently assistant to the rector, said, "He was doing his thing. The presence and image he projected—the authority—actually was different from the real man, because basically, I was to find out later, he is a shy man. Personal contact can be hard for him. But he sure didn't show it then."

"He was terrific," said Betty March. "He had real authority. He was intelligent, and he was humorous. He was just *good*."

But there were detractors, those who winced, those who flushed angrily. "I thought he came on too strong," said one man. "I felt he was pretty presumptuous," said another. "He sure indicated he was going to lay it on the line," concluded a third. Few were ambivalent.

Fullam pressed his case that morning by examining what those who knew Jesus during His ministry and right afterward had had to say about Him.

"When we try to find out something about a man we usually go to those who know him best," he said. "Since I do not want to be partial I will want to go to His enemies as well as His friends. And I would like to ask them all the very same question: 'What think ye of Christ?' "

He began with the Pharisees and led his audience through to what they said of Him—*"this man receives sinners."*[5]

"Isn't it marvelous," summarized Fullam, "that the very worst thing the Pharisees could say about Him was to point out His marvelous grace which He extends to us in forgiving our sins?

"But that's not all they said," he added quickly. "They also said, *'He saved others; himself he cannot save.'*[6] And again they were right, absolutely right. Isn't it strange

---

[5]Luke 15:2.   [6]Mark 15:31.

and yet wonderful that the very worst thing their hatred could find to say was to point in magnificent eloquence to the matchless grace of Jesus Christ and His willingness to lay down His own life that you and I might live?"

Then he turned to Pontius Pilate and took them through to the point where Jesus was brought before the Roman procurator. "And as you all know, Pilate finally gave in to the crowd," he said softly, "but not before he bore this testimony: 'I find *no fault* in him.' "[7]

He paused to let the six words settle. "Do you remember an incident that occurred at the very same time? While the trial was going on somebody came in and gave Pilate a note from his wife. And the note said, 'Have nothing to do with that *just man*: for I have suffered many things this day in a dream because of him.' "[8]

Then came Judas, following his tragic conspiracy: "I have sinned in betraying *innocent* blood."[9]

And the thief on the cross: "This man has done nothing amiss."[10]

Fullam spoke deliberately, movingly, of the Roman centurion charged with carrying out the crucifixion—one who had heard Jesus say, as the nails were pounded through His hands and feet, "Father, forgive them, for they know not what they do." This centurion spoke at last, "Surely this was *the Son of God!*"[11]

"Well, here you have it," Terry said soberly, fully open-faced. "You have the combined testimony of the enemies of Jesus Christ. Listen to it:

" 'This man receives sinners.'

" 'He saved others; himself he cannot save.'

" 'I find no fault in him.'

" 'Have nothing to do with that just man.'

" 'I have sinned in betraying innocent blood.'

" 'This man has done nothing amiss.'

" 'Surely this was the Son of God.' "

---

[7]John 18:38.　　　[8]Matthew 27:19.　　　[9]Matthew 27:4.　　　[10]Luke 23:41
[11]Matthew 27:54.

He then smiled widely, but softly. "Again, isn't it strange and yet marvelous that the testimony of the enemies of Jesus so magnificently lays before us the grace and the glory of the Son of God?"

He waited, knowing that even the wincers and the flushers were intent. Not a smirk was visible.

"But consider His friends for a moment," he continued, moving quickly into a recitation of what several other Bible figures had to say about Jesus.

First, there was the statement of John the Baptist: "Behold, the Lamb of God, who takes away the sin of the world!"[12]

He followed with Peter: "You are the Christ, the Son of the living God."[13]

Suddenly, almost magically, the pulse of the service quickened; the atmosphere seemed to thin; upturned faces stretched taut. The words flowed effortlessly from Fullam, and no one seemed any longer concerned with "authority" or "presence." They were absorbed in content.

Lift up your eyes a moment, to the very courts of heaven itself. Can you see the throne of God—and gathered around the throne the great ransomed host of all the ages? St. John tells us what they would say if we put the question to them: "Who is Christ? What think ye of Him?"

Can you hear the chorus? "Worthy is the Lamb who was slain, to receive power and wealth and wisdom and might and honor and glory and blessing!"[14]

But there's one other story I want you to hear—one other answer to this question, "What think ye of Christ?" In a way, it's the most important one of all.

---

[12]John 1:29.   [13]Matthew 16:16.   [14]Revelation 5:12.

Come with me, if you will, with Peter and James and John to a little elevation and there, before our very eyes, see the Lord Jesus Christ transfigured—transformed. For one brief moment, we are allowed to see Him with the glory which He had with the Father before the world began. We see Him as He really is, not as He disguised himself when He entered humbly into this world as a babe. We see Him as the mighty King and God that He is.

And listen. For while we are looking at Him in rapt attention, there comes a voice from heaven, "This is my beloved Son: hear him."[15]

Now for one brief moment, put out of your mind any distraction. Don't think of the people sitting around. Don't think of the fact that this is my first Sunday here with you. Put these things out of your mind if you can. And *hear* Him.

And what does He say? "Come to me, all who labor and are heavy laden, and I will give you rest."[16]

Jesus says, "I am come that they might have life and . . . have it more abundantly."[17]

Jesus says, I am come "that your joy may be full."[18]

Jesus says, "My peace I give unto you."[19]

Life, joy, and peace—the three things perhaps that the world wants more than anything else—are offered to us through Jesus Christ, do you see?

Perhaps you think this is a strange message and wonder why I have chosen this as my first sermon to you. Well, it's not simply because this question appears in today's Gospel—though it does—but it is because one of the things that impressed me about this church was the announced goal "to know Christ and to make Him known."[20] And, of course, we cannot do that unless together we answer this question: "What think ye of Christ? Whose Son is

---

[15]Mark 9:7.   [16]Matthew 11:28.   [17]John 10:10.
[18]John 15:11.   [19]John 14:27.   [20]See chapter five.

He?"

Oh, yes, you've been asked in your lifetime many important questions, I do not doubt. But none are as important as this question. For on this question, "What think ye of Christ?" depends not only the possibility of fullness of life now, but the gift of eternal life hereafter.

Mastery of the Bible

A student and teacher of philosophy and logic, one who early in life perceived within himself the ability to make others see and understand complex truths and concepts through the examination of their often simple component strands, Fullam that very first day turned his main thrust into a full circle and made it complete. The people *saw*—perhaps through cobwebs in some cases. Their questions had been answered, even though they basically had been left with a question.

He had immediately revealed the capacity to foresee any question that might arise about his subject. And moments after a listener—myself included—might say to himself something like, "Aha, Terry, but what about so-and-so; how do you account for that?" he would answer that very question.

To many, it might have seemed arrogant, but I found it entirely humble and honest when, over dinner, I once heard him say, "No question ever catches me by surprise. I've been asked so many, many thousands of questions over the years—especially by my students—that I almost never hear a question for the first time now. And, of course, that enables me to head a lot of them off ahead of time."

It was a simple explanation, but I think perhaps a bit too modest. As I sat listening to Terry from time to time in those early days—traveling some distance from my home in Westchester County—I, with hundreds of others, marveled at his ability to organize his material so thoroughly and to present it almost flawlessly without a note, without even a heavily marked-up Bible. He did believe in marking up a Bible—and urged his parishioners to do so—but there inevitably came the time when, in his rather disorganized manner, he lost his fairly worn, red-leather Revised Standard Version and had to obtain another quickly. He went through a lot of Bibles this way. The new one—blue leather—naturally was unmarked, no underlining, no marginal notes, no creased pages at key passages. And right from the beginning, he preached and taught impeccably from it. Zip, zip, zip to this New Testament verse. Zap, zap, zap to that Old Testament principle.

I've encountered a few other men and women over the years whose Bible mastery was phenomenal. As you watched them go from subject to subject, you could almost hear the click-click-clicking of their brains, like computers. But with Terry it was soundless, smooth, well-oiled—almost too effortless, I thought; it must be supernatural.

But Terry showed something else that very first day. It came in the prayer that closed his sermon. Few grasped the prophetic undercurrent in the ninety words spoken spontaneously and earnestly by the tall professor turned parish priest. But hindsight showed he spoke as a prophet.

The prayer began pretty much as a standard, Episcopal-sounding entreaty, even with the conventional "let us pray," followed by the rather awkward pause and shuffling of feet and banging of kneelers, as the one hundred seventy-five men and women eased or creaked or groaned into a kneeling position and let loose a number of pent-up coughs. Fullam's voice was strong and clear:

Lord Jesus, we pray that you will somehow give us ears to hear, hearts to love, and wills devoted to serve; that in the days to come this congregation may be known, not for our glory, but for thine alone—a congregation of people who know the Lord; that this place may be an oasis, a place where people come to find out about you, where lives are straightened out and made whole, where people find the peace that passes understanding. Give us, we pray, a heart to desire these things above all else. We pray through Jesus Christ. Amen.

Be What You Are

From his first days at St. Paul's—even in the first six months when he returned to Providence for three days each week to fulfill his teaching agreement at Barrington—Fullam treated his congregation like mature, committed Christians, which was not always the case. One subtle, yet significant example occurred, and still does, at each Sunday service. It would come during his greeting of the people, when with a radiant, tender smile he would spread wide his arms and joyfully say something like: "Beloved of the Lord Jesus, people of God's delight, members of the household of God, and saints called into the fellowship of the Holy Spirit!" Or it might be: "Good Christian people, welcome in the name of the Lord Jesus Christ."

His words were forever positive and his manner consistently encouraging. He lifted the people, merely in the way he treated them. It was as though he were saying to them: "You say you are God's people and I will treat you as God's people; *be* what you are."

His manner breathed personal assurance into the apostle Paul's declaration in Romans 8: "There is therefore now no condemnation for those who are in Christ Jesus." The people were able to believe it.

And, although it took several weeks for this to be perceived, Fullam's teaching, counseling, and attitude never communicated the idea that one *must* do this, or one *should* do that, or one *ought* to stop doing so-and-so. His practice was to show what the Scripture said, to tell the people to seek what God wanted them to do, and to pray that the Holy Spirit would enable them. He seemed to see his role as one of constantly pointing toward God and encouraging the people to yield themselves to Him. I have known few men or women who had as much faith in God's ability and willingness to lead people who submitted themselves to Him. He said many times, "God desires for you to do His will far more than you desire to do it."

Fundamentals Without Fundamentalism

Basic Christianity—basic principles—flowed through the sanctuary and meeting rooms in those early days. Fundamentals were expounded, but not fundamentalism with its pejorative, twentieth-century connotations. Understanding was enlarged, faith was heightened.

"The resurrection of Jesus Christ is the central reality in the life of believing people," Fullam declared one Sunday from the pulpit. "It is to be *experienced*. And those who experience it experience new life *now*."

The teaching on faith in Christ, the forgiveness of sins, and eternal life was strong and solid, but the reality of the Christian life *now* was an even stronger theme. First came the underlying Scripture: "And you he made alive, when you were dead through the trespasses and sins in which you once walked, following the course of this world, following the prince of the power of the air, the spirit that is now at work in the sons of disobedience."[21]

Then came the background, the seeing of oneself: "Now

---

[21]Ephesians 2:1-2.

in order to understand that extraordinary statement, we must go back to the Garden of Eden. Do you remember the Lord God saying to Adam and Eve, 'In the day that you eat thereof you shall surely die'?[22] Now the fact of the matter is that when they disobeyed the Lord and partook of the forbidden fruit, they did not in fact die physically that day. But they died spiritually, *for man was created for fellowship with almighty God—and that's what died that day.*

"They were afraid," he explained carefully and patiently. "A new emotion came into their hearts they had never experienced before. Fear. And they went and hid themselves. They were afraid because they had died. The one with whom they walked freely in the garden was somehow now an enemy, and they were dead. The Scripture [he lifted his Bible up above his shoulder] all the way through makes the same point, that in our natural condition we are dead toward God."

Many in the congregation and those at the weeknight Bible studies had been fairly well-grounded in historic Christianity, but many had not. So always there was a mixture of nodding concurrence and open-mouthed absorption in comprehending at last the condition of man.

Fullam dealt graphically with that condition. "We come into the world believing somehow that we are the center of the universe, that everything exists somehow to minister to our desires and our needs. Sometimes we manage to cloak this and mask it so as to get along better with people, but let us not fool ourselves: *At the heart of man is an incurable desire to be first and to be central.* Somehow we want to twist other people around until they minister to our needs. Somehow we want to control things so as to accomplish our purpose. It's innate. It's natural. It's doing what comes naturally. That's the human circumstance."

---

[22]Genesis 2:17.

Many heads nodded. Many ironic smiles accompanied lowered eyes.

But Fullam moved quickly to lift his congregation. His voice was especially clear, tenorlike; his face unsmiling, but optimistic. "Now the Scripture tells us from that state of spiritual deadness we have to be made alive. We have to have a resurrection. There are, as we've seen, two kinds of death, physical death and spiritual death. But there are also two kinds of life."

Here he smiled briefly. "There is natural life that you and I derive from our parents, and there is spiritual life."

At this point he turned to St. John's account of Jesus' encounter with Nicodemus (chapter 3), which provides much of the understanding of the "born-again" experience.

"You'll recall," Fullam said, once again giving his listeners the benefit of the doubt, "Jesus said, 'Nicodemus, in order to see the kingdom of heaven you must be born again.'"

He paused very slightly. "In other words, Jesus said, to be a Christian, to be a follower of His, was such a radically new thing, that it's like starting life all over again. You must be born again. It's saying the same thing, you see. It's starting life afresh. It's a new look. It's life transposed now into a new key. *Here we are to be raised from deadness into life in our relationship to almighty God.*"

And then, in the manner of the good professor, came the *how*. "But, you might say, how does a person pass from spiritual death to spiritual life?"

Once again, to the Scripture. "In the letter to the Colossians, this is what we read: ' . . . and you were buried with him (Jesus) in baptism, in which you were also raised with him *through faith* in the working of God, who raised him from the dead.' "[23]

An explanation of tradition, immediately another

---

[23]Colossians 2:12.

Fullam trademark, came next. He told how Holy Saturday had become the traditional time for baptisms in the Christian Church—the day between Good Friday and Easter, observing the time when Jesus was buried. "Now the reason for that is very clear"—again, the confidence, the trust in the Scripture. "It's because we are *baptized into the death of Christ.*[24] Something in us has to die."

Once more came the illustration, the imagery, that steadily brought the Bible and its principles to life for the people who for the most part had taken only a few tentative steps, if any, toward the depth of the Scripture:

> But we are also to emerge into the newness of life that is symbolized by Jesus' resurrection from the dead. Something new comes into being.
>
> But did you get the wording of this? It's very important. We were *baptized into his death.* Now we can do that to one another. We can take a child, and I can baptize that child into the *death* of Jesus Christ, but that's as far as I can go. For then we read, "and you were raised with him *through faith in the working of God,* who raised him from the dead."
>
> The trouble with hundreds, maybe thousands, of Christian people today is that they have indeed been baptized into the death of Christ. They have been buried under the water, as it were, *and they're still there*, swimming around under water.
>
> But, you see, in order to come to newness of life they must come *by faith in the Lord Jesus Christ.* If the Scripture is clear about anything, it is clear about that. *Nobody can be saved by what another person can do to them.* I can perform rituals for you. I can say words over you. I can utter prayers in your behalf. *But it must be that all-personal faith arising in the Lord Jesus Christ that brings you out of the*

[24]Romans 6:3.

72

waters of death into the new life of the resurrection.

This was plain and unusual talk for an Episcopal church in the early seventies, especially one situated among a population weaned on the subtleties of relativism, materialism, and self-righteousness. But to those paying close attention there was a perceptible current at work in the stream of new light flowing in their midst. It was a current that brushed, even pounded, against some of the pillars and foundations of their beloved Anglican tradition, but it did not destroy. It cleansed and illuminated, adding meaning and restoring beauty. It slowly turned ritual into life.

A Different Objective
The steady movement forward continued—personal movement, individual awakening, the encouragement of faith. There was more than new life right now, Fullam said. There was something else to be experienced.

"We experience *a new walk* right now," he declared. He allowed several moments for the idea to sink in. Then came the breezy sound of rapidly moving sheets of India paper as he again led the people into their Bibles. This time it was Romans 6:4: "We were buried therefore with him by baptism into death, so that as Christ was raised from the dead by the glory of the Father, we too might *walk* in newness of life."

He put down his Bible. "You see, something happens. The Christian life is to be a different life. We are raised to a new level, transposed into another key. That's what it's talking about. *We are to walk in newness of life.*"

Back up came the Bible. "It's put in slightly different words later on in the chapter. 'But if we have died with Christ, we believe that we shall also live *with* him.'[25] Do you see? To walk in newness of life is to walk and to live

---
[25]Romans 6:8.

with the Lord Jesus Christ."

Again, a pause for absorption. "And a bit further down it's put still another way: 'So you also must consider yourselves *dead* to sin and *alive* to God in Christ Jesus.'[26] So, you see, the new life that we receive is to issue in a new walk, *a walk with Jesus*, a walk unto the Lord, in which we live our lives unto God and unto the praise and glory of God who created us."

But there was a third thing to be experienced in the resurrection. It was *a new goal, a new objective, to life.* Quickly, Terry eased his congregation back into the Bible. They were beginning to get used to it.

"We've been in Romans," he said; "now turn right to Colossians." It was a line—"turn right" or "turn left"—that was to bring smiles to faces pressed into Bibles over the months and years.

"St. Paul describes it in these words," he said, lifting his Bible, " 'If then you have been raised with Christ, *seek the things that are above*, where Christ is, seated at the right hand of God. *Set your minds on things that are above*, not on things that are on earth.' "[27]

He tucked the Bible under his arm. "A new goal, a new objective. If you be raised with Christ then seek those things which are above. That's St. Paul's way of saying what Jesus said in the Sermon on the Mount: 'Seek ye first the kingdom of God, and his righteousness; and all these things shall be added unto you.'[28]

"So, you see, Christian living, resurrection living, is living according to priority—the priority of seeking first the kingdom of God."

His face opened wide and the merest trace of a smile crept onto his lips. " 'But,' you say, 'what is the kingdom of God?' Jesus, in the Lord's Prayer, said, 'Thy kingdom come, thy will be done on earth, as it is in heaven.'[29] He equates the coming of the kingdom with doing the will of

---

[26]Romans 6:11.   [27]Colossians 3:1-2.   [28]Matthew 6:33, KJV.
[29]Matthew 6:10.

God. Experiencing the kingdom of God is *doing the will of God.* Jesus said, concerning himself, 'I have not come to do my own will; I have come to do the will of my Father';[30] 'I do not do what I desire,' He said; 'I do only such things as I am directed by the Father.'

"And you will find that one of the characteristics of the new life experience, the new life walked in, will be a desire to live our lives according to the will of God. His purpose for us will become supremely important. His plan for our life will be our quest and discovery. The accomplishing of the good works that He has prepared for us to walk in[31] will become the magnificent obsession of all who experience the resurrection."

A Pattern Emerges

A lay reader in the church, Phil March, a man of considerable experience in worship and in ministry, saw immediately the pattern that emerged in the early weeks of Fullam's work at St. Paul's.

"First of all," he said, "you have to remember that Terry had pretty much everything going for him right from the beginning. A good foundation of interest in the deeper things of God had been laid by Art Lane and others during those first years. There were no serious divisions in the church. And there was nothing shabby. Everything was first class."

And into that scene strode the hulking professor-philosopher-priest from northern New England. "What we had then," March continued, "was the traditional people coming to the Lord and getting baptized in the Holy Spirit—the people who had sort of played around in the Episcopal church most of their lives—they more or less figured, 'Well, we've got it all' and then they discovered something was lacking and Fullam was able to help them find it. That was really the thing

---

[30]John 6:38.   [31]Ephesians 2:10.

that impressed me in those early days—seeing the old-line church people gradually, or sometimes suddenly, come awake to the fact that Jesus was alive and they were supposed to be involved with Him. And, of course, you had the new people coming at the same time, the people who had really wanted nothing to do with an established church, but who were finding that this guy was making good sense, even to some sophisticated Madison Avenue type in the twentieth century, and they wanted to come and find out what it was about. And then they got zapped, and before you knew it, they were coming because they really wanted to.

"So," he concluded with a smile, "you had a lot of the old people coming alive, really for the first time, and then the new ones, who were being exposed for the first time. It was a double-edged revival."

When a new rector comes to a church, there are inevitably jealousies and often some grumbling. Most of the time, it involves those who were on the inside in the old guard and with the changing of that guard find themselves on the outside with their noses pressed against the window glass like little children looking wistfully in at all the merriment.

And then, there are those who just like to grumble, and even gossip.

From the beginning of the new wave of God's move upon the church of St. Paul's, this kind of activity was at a minimum. Mainly this was because the classifications of "insider" and "outsider" were studiously avoided. Everything was open to everyone. Nothing was restricted, and that fact was well publicized.

But there were times when grumbles threatened to rise above a whisper. Often they sprang from jealousy or frightened egos—frequently beginning with sarcasm and escalating to envy.

On one of Fullam's first Sundays as rector, the first whiffs of jealousy were detected. Not everyone knew that this formidable teacher was nearly as imposing musically. He was talented and thoroughly schooled. He could perform, he could teach, and he could compose.

On that Sunday Fullam arranged for one of the choir's outstanding sopranos to perform a song related to the text he was to preach from. He had written the song. When the service reached the point for the solo, the rector walked to the far left of the altar area, and with a sweep of his robe, seated himself at the organ and played a beautiful, delicate introduction and accompaniment for the soloist.

One man admitted later to having turned to his companion and whispered loudly enough for others to hear, "I guess this guy will be taking up the offering next."

Versatility can be intimidating.

"I liked him," said another member of the church, "but I was jealous of him."

Not All Will Come

Bishop Alexander Stewart's words were as fresh as the day they were spoken years earlier when Terry stepped into the pulpit the second Sunday of his St. Paul's ministry. (There was disagreement among several old-timers as to whether this was the first, second, or third Sunday, but the second seemed to have the most reliable evidence.) "Nobody can minister to everybody," the western Massachusetts bishop had said when he was Terry's rector in Rhode Island. "Not even Jesus did."

It was sound advice, and Terry did not forget it. He felt the Lord had made clear that he was to move forward with those he was given. He was not to worry about those not yet ready to move along or those who did not understand. He was not to cut anyone off, but neither was he to let anyone hold him back. God would bring in whom He wanted; that was what a church was. God's purpose from Adam onward was to develop a people who would voluntarily respond to Him and move under His leading. He had always sought a people who would obey Him. Down through history He had found groups here and there, but never was the obedience perfect. Never was the understanding complete.

That second Sunday, Fullam stood erect and still in the pulpit. As before, one hundred seventy-five pairs of eyes watched him intently. He was still something of a curiosity.

"I think it's important for all of us to realize something," he began. "In the coming months, one of two things will happen to each one of you."

Expectancy tightened. "Either you will find yourself opening up more and more to the Lord, in which case you will be growing and expanding in your relationship with Him—and you will know it—or else you will find yourself constricting and tightening, in which case the atmosphere will become intolerable."

The silence was absolute.

"Some of you will find it necessary to go."

Everything held still for a second, then emotions spun off into directions that would not be clearly defined for some time.

The word of the Lord spoken in the power of the Holy Spirit changes lives. It has always been so. It would be so there. It would be impossible for the people to come into the sanctuary and sit in those pews week after week, with any degree of openness, and not be changed—one way or the other. Fullam knew that. History supported it. But which way would it be with the people of Darien?

PART TWO:

THE PRINCIPLES

CHAPTER FIVE

Eight Words

It seems that God looks around for a man or a woman
with ears to hear what He's saying and a willingness to do
what He's saying before He ever undertakes a work. Of
course, because God is sovereign and knows the
beginning from the end, it doesn't really work that way.
He doesn't stumble along, hoping He can get something
done, and then suddenly see someone who seems to be
obedient, snapping His fingers and saying something like,
"Son of a gun, what a surprise! That may be my man!"

No, things do not catch God by surprise. But still, it
looks that way sometimes. He seems first to find His man
or woman, and second to lay out a set of principles for the
people, and then to say, "Now work them out."

It would appear that God had found His man for what
He wanted to do in Darien. But, He had also been setting
up a platform for the receipt of His principles. In fact, God
had gotten quite a bit ahead of everyone by laying down
the first and very crucial principle even before the teacher
from Barrington College had come into anyone else's
sight. And it is necessary to go back to that point for a few
moments to glimpse the fullness of the miracle in Darien.

H. Arthur Lane was essentially a kind and loving man who responded to a call to the ordained ministry as a mature adult. He was dark-haired and rather slight, immediately striking a visitor with his quietness, maybe even shyness, in his Darien days. As the St. Paul's congregation's second clergyman, he arrived in 1966 in succession to William Bartlett, who was returning to seminary. Bartlett, an organizer and builder, had come as vicar when St. Luke's Church in Darien started St. Paul's as a mission in 1960, in the days when the twenty-five or so families met as a chapel in the Hollow Tree School. He became the moving force in the drive to build the present Mansfield Avenue building.

Virtually everyone in a position of knowledge agreed that Father Lane was the perfect pastor for those fragile days when the spiritual staging was being pieced together at St. Paul's. He was not the impressive preacher or gifted musician that God would ultimately call forth, but his qualities were those highly treasured by the Lord, love and compassion, the ones that work when all else fails.

Ed Ferree, also a kindly, soft-spoken man, whose gentleness often masks extraordinary organizational skill, probably summed up the St. Paul's old-timers' view of Lane better than anyone else. He used only eleven words: "He was a loving person—someone who made everyone feel loved."

Mike McManus added a dimension he had picked up as a reporter, even though he wasn't present at the time: "He had an excitement about studying the Scriptures that was infectious."

And that turned out to be significant.

In the late sixties, Lane started a Bible study in his living room for Sunday school teachers. Four people attended—a rather classic Episcopal response to the study of the Bible. But Lane wasn't bound by numbers; he persisted. And by 1972, fifty to seventy people were gathering weekly to study and discuss the Bible and to pray, having shifted the meeting time to Wednesday night.

The platform could almost be seen taking shape.

By 1970, Lane was asking a most pointed question—first of himself and then of others. He eventually posed it to the vestry, with a recommendation that it be considered seriously.

"What is it we are trying to do at St. Paul's?" he asked simply. Most faces were blank at first. Many vestrymen looked from one to the other, and back to Lane.

"What is our purpose?" he pressed on. "What is our purpose, stated succinctly?"

The discussion was on, and it continued for several weeks. The vestry debated the matter more than once. "He forced us to face up to the fact that we had no clear goal," Carl Rodemann said sometime later.

Finally, they came up with a statement:

The purpose of St. Paul's Church is to bring people to know Jesus Christ personally, and to advance and strengthen the love of God and Man—as taught by Christ—within our family, parish, community and to all men everywhere.

"Not bad," everyone said, with a pursing of the lips and a nod of the head. "Not bad at all."

But still—and most eventually agreed on this—it was quite a mouthful. It was good, but hadn't Arthur used the word "succinct"? It really wasn't succinct.

So they kept polishing it, and kicking it around, and finally got it down to just eight words:

To know Christ and to make Him known.

The pursed lips parted into wide smiles. "That's it." They all knew it. The eight little words stuck—to this day.

Hammering out a statement of purpose may have been as important as anything that was done at St. Paul's, at least in those first years. Just the process of exploration and hard thinking was good for those involved. "It was a healthy exercise," said Rodemann, "sort of like zero-base budgeting." They peeled away everything and went right down to the essentials.

And then when they had articulated the result, they found strength in merely knowing their basic objective. They began to measure their activities by that objective. They had a yardstick. "Does this program help us to know Christ better or does it help us to make Him known to others?" If it didn't, it had to be set aside, at least eventually.

As a result, the time soon came when St. Paul's parish held none of the usual bazaars, church sales, and fairs. It had no book review clubs, no investment clubs, no primarily cultural activities. It wasn't that these things were bad in themselves; they just didn't fall within the definition of purpose. They could be done far better elsewhere.

At last, the fledgling church had a vision of its goal. Now it would know if it hit that goal or not.

CHAPTER SIX

The Head

He is the head of the body, the church.[1]

Sitting in a restaurant over an early-morning meal of pancakes, eggs, and bacon, Fullam reflected on his first days among the people of St. Paul's Church.

"The thing that was so firmly impressed upon me was that I was to establish the headship of Christ over them—because the church was His body, and He could do nothing unless His headship was recognized."

He took a drink of orange juice from the tall, amber glass. "If it was recognized, He'd do it all. That was very clear. That was part of the Sinai—to establish His headship over them, and He would do it all. And He was going to lead me, and I was going to lead them. But they were going to have to see, and live as though, He was the head."

He shifted his weight to lean into the corner of the booth. "You see, the Lord made it very clear that I was to expend a considerable amount of effort—all it would take—to establish that reality in the life of this congregation."

That was the key. *Establish that reality in life*. The

---

[1]Colossians 1:18.

words spoke light to events at St. Paul's. *Becoming what we say we believe*—that was a clue.

In the first two-thirds of the seventies, American evangelical and charismatic Christians heard much preaching and teaching on the lordship of Christ. One of the favorite renewal songs was "He Is Lord." Many began to think of Jesus as king; they grappled with concepts of sovereignty as well as the great high priesthood. From chapter twenty-eight, verse eighteen, of St. Matthew's Gospel came a favorite Scripture quotation: "All authority in heaven and on earth has been given to me."

But how was this to become reality in a congregation?

Besides his encounter with the Lord at Mount Sinai, Fullam depended heavily on the words of Jesus as recorded in Matthew 16:18. In the passage, Peter has just confessed that Jesus is "the Christ, the Son of the living God," and the Lord makes it plain that on those who make such a confession, *He* will build *His* Church. And He adds powerfully and conclusively that the Gates of Hell, the Gates of Hades, the powers of death "shall not prevail against it."

Additionally, Terry leaned strongly on the New Testament's repeated declarations that *Jesus is the head of His body*, which is the Church.

"The trouble," he said in many variations, "is that much of the Church, even that part which openly acknowledges that the Scripture says Jesus is the head, does not really act as though it believes He is capable of running that of which He is the head. They seem to think somebody else has to run it."

This seemed to be particularly true in the Episcopal church. The feeling was especially strong that the rector was the head of the local church. A lot of this strong feeling, quite naturally, could be traced to the Episcopal structure. The priest was vested, by order and tradition as well, with unusual authority. He was the only one who could speak, especially on "spiritual" matters, and get anyone to listen to him. If it didn't come through him, it wasn't authoritative.

Thus many had difficulty handling teaching which said that the church was a body headed by Christ and that the rector was merely one of many members of that body. True, the teaching went, the rector had authority as an overseer. He was a leader, a shepherd perhaps—a functionary—but he was not the *head* of the church. Jesus was the head. Jesus worked through him, and others, in the manner that the brain worked through a mouth, an eye, or an arm. But the mouth, the eye, and the arm were *not* the brain.

"I am *not* the head of this church," Fullam said over and over. At first, many smiled and nodded. Some even thought and said such things as "Isn't that nice? Isn't that humble and thoughtful?" But few immediately grasped the idea that he meant it.

"I can't build this church," he declared. "I haven't the foggiest idea how to do it. But the Lord knows how, and He will do it if we just submit ourselves to Him. He is perfectly capable of building His own church."

It is difficult for a group of individuals, particularly a group of talented, naturally gifted individuals, to submit to absolute direction. And it is doubly difficult when that absolute direction is to come from someone you can't see—someone you know is there only by faith since you haven't had time to build much visible evidence.

"This sounds good," many at St. Paul's said under their breath or softly to trusted friends, "but how in heck is it going to work? What does he mean when he says Jesus will direct us?"

As I touched on earlier, Terry has a rare method of getting people to perceive the Lord's leading. He described it that early morning in the restaurant.

"There are two or three words I never use: 'should' or 'ought.' The moment I say, 'You should do this,' I am laying law on you. I'm putting you under an obligation, at least as I see it."

He paused, and looked intently at his hands, which he had raised to the table in front of him. "I'm so convinced that it's a *gospel of grace* that we're talking about, and that I really should, rather than tell you you *should* do this or you *shouldn't* do that—I should tell you to yield yourself to the Holy Spirit. Because if you really were yielded, and He wanted to do something, He'd put it in your head to do it and you'd really want to."

He looked up again, and smiled. "And that's the law written on the heart. That's the new covenant in place of the old covenant."

We were both silent a moment. And then he continued rather softly, "So, although I received a revelation at Sinai, it was a revelation of grace, not of law. I think that's important. St. Paul's has been singularly free from the legalisms that I think have marred so many other groups. We don't try to put people under the law. We're willing to wait and let the Lord show them the way. I really believe that if we just let the people come in and seek the Lord, they will find His way. And so will we, as a body. I just assume that whoever is there is a candidate for what the Lord is doing."

An important teaching in this concept of allowing Jesus to run the church is found in Christ's description of one of the activities of the Holy Spirit. It is recorded among the five passages in chapters 14-16 of St. John's Gospel that provide major teachings in the words of the Lord on the Holy Spirit. In chapter 16:12-15, Jesus is quoted as follows:

> I have yet many things to say to you, but you cannot bear them now. When the Spirit of truth comes, *he will guide you into all the truth;* for he will not speak on his own authority, but whatever he hears he will speak, and he will declare to you the things that are to come. He will glorify me, for *he will take what is mine and declare it to you.* All that the Father has is mine; therefore I said that he will take what is mine and declare it to you.

That is a clear description of a significant part of the work of the Spirit: to glorify the Lord Jesus Christ and to reveal the things, the works, of Christ. He will, as it were, reveal *what Christ is doing.* The Holy Spirit, then, is very selfless. His job is to make Jesus real to the Lord's followers.

This immediately reminds one of earlier words of Jesus, also recorded in John 5:19, 20. There Jesus described *His* role as a selfless one. He was to reveal the Father, to do His work. It was almost as though He were doing to the Father what the Holy Spirit was to do to Jesus.

> Jesus said to them, "Truly, truly, I say to you, the Son can do nothing of his own accord, but only what *he sees the Father doing; for whatever he does, that the Son does likewise.* For the Father loves the Son, and *shows him all that he himself is doing. . . ."*

The task of Jesus was to see what the Father was doing.

The task of the follower of Jesus is to see what Jesus is doing. Jesus stayed totally under the lordship of the Father. The Christian must stay under the lordship of Jesus. In both cases, the Holy Spirit makes this possible. He is the working arm of the godhead on earth, being the only member of the Trinity who is here at this time.

Very practically, the Christian—or a group of Christians, a church—should be continually looking, by means of the Holy Spirit, to see what Jesus is doing and thereby perceiving what he should be doing. In this manner, through prayer and communion with the Lord, he understands God's will, as Jesus understood the Father's will.

And this is what God is looking for, in an individual and in the church—people who *will* to do His will, people who are constantly looking to see if they are under His lordship, His headship.

"Lo, I am with you always, to the close of the age."[2] The words return over and over, daily.

A Layman Tells It

Carl Rodemann, a former senior warden, is an open-faced man with an easy smile and twinkling, crinkly-cornered eyes, but behind them, ready when needed, are a strength and toughness of mind, the confidence of a leader. He spoke casually and lightly to the sanctuary full of visitors from other towns during one of St. Paul's parish renewal weekends.

"And I want to restate," he said carefully, "that we are not trying to tell anyone else how they should run their church, but we're only trying to share our experiences."

It was hard to believe, while listening to him that morning, that not long before he had been virtually unable to stand before a gathering of that size and speak so clearly and easily about matters of the Lord, because of

---

[2]Matthew 28:20.

uncertainty and ignorance. But that morning he had something to give.

He continued, "And some of the techniques may be useful to you and some not at all. Some may be transferrable and others definitely should be left here. But we feel that, underlying the techniques and the practices, the procedures, and the events, there are some principles, and that these principles are universal and available and important to every church body everywhere."

His twinkling eyes swept across the sanctuary. "The first one is that Jesus is head of this church—not the rector, and that may come as a surprise to some people; not the senior warden, and that's equally surprising to others; not any group of large contributors, or any other individual or group."

Again, his eyes moved across the room. "But Jesus is the head. And we have learned that this very simple statement is an enormously profound one and has absolutely shattering implications if really understood and applied."

His voice rose ever so slightly and his tempo quickened. "It's His kingdom we are building, not our own. And it's His power that will do it, not our own."

I shifted in the pew to try to get a better look at Terry off to the side a few rows back from the front. I couldn't see his face directly, but I could tell by the lines in his cheek that he was smiling. The lesson that Rodemann spoke so succinctly and sincerely had not been an easy one to get across in the beginning. It was contrary to the nature of man, particularly men and women accustomed to decision-making and leadership, as many of the privileged people of the Darien area were.

Interestingly, it was Rodemann, that very morning, who captured the difficulty in an interlude. Again, the corners of his eyes crinkled and a smile played at the corners of his mouth:

"It reminds me of a story I heard a few weeks ago. It seems the parish had a new rector, and he came and he preached his first sermon on the subject of *Love*. And afterwards everyone filed out and said to him, 'That was an outstanding sermon . . . brilliant . . . the best ever' . . . etc.

"The next Sunday everybody came to church and, lo and behold, he preached the same sermon identically. And people were puzzled. But then they said to themselves, 'Well, it was so good and really so well done, it probably was worth hearing twice.'

"The third Sunday, the same sermon on Love, and everyone became sort of quiet. The fourth Sunday, when this happened again, why, the senior warden headed a committee, a delegation, that went to see the rector. And they said, 'Look, we know that's a good sermon, and we know you're pretty proud of it, we know you like it, but don't you have another one?' "

Rodemann paused to set the stage. His smile widened. "To which the new rector replied, 'Yes, I do. And as soon as you learn the first one, I'll start on another.' "

And that's the way it went at St. Paul's, although Fullam never resorted to the repetition of a sermon. But he pounded at his theme from every direction—from all the Scripture, from early church history, from personal experience.

"Jesus is the head of the church."

"Jesus can run the church."

Music and Worship

"Music is a super-important part of his ministry," said Phil March, who watched Fullam closely from the beginning of his Darien work. "With it, plus his own personality and his sort of built-in authority, he has an unusual ability to break the ice and get people to worshiping the Lord and really enjoying it. He makes it seem okay."

To many observers, that was perhaps *the* vital key to the exploding growth at St. Paul's: music and worship. They went hand in hand, almost as one, and flowed perfectly with the relentless emphasis on the lordship of Christ. Jesus, the head, was to be worshiped.

The worship became almost as central to the life in the church as the preaching of the Word. And this included the Sunday services, the mushrooming Wednesday night Bible studies, and essentially every event in the church. Even business meetings had a brief time set apart for worship.

Rodemann explained it well. "We believe that we were called to be a worshiping fellowship. And we believe that this includes teaching people to worship—teaching people to open themselves up to a joyful and expressive worship, worship where people can enter in with warmth and vigor. We believe it is good to have balance between structure and spontaneity, between authority and freedom."

That sounded good, even for Episcopalians. And Fullam made it even more attractive for them, or anyone else.

"Now it is true that right from the days of the apostles the worship of the Christians centered in the Lord's Supper," he said. "And this was basically the only form of worship that they had for the first nearly sixteen hundred years of the Christian church. After the sixteenth century, the Protestant Reformation, another kind of worship came into being that is characteristic of many Protestant communions. But what goes on in an average Protestant church on a Sunday morning would not be recognized for the first thousand years or so in the Christian church as a service of Christian worship."

As always, when he so clearly related today's practices to those of history and explored the meanings behind traditions, his listeners became very still, rapt and expectant.

"Not that there is anything wrong with it," he went on, "but simply that it represented a rather significant change, because Christian worship always, right from the very first, on the pages of the New Testament, centered in the Lord's Supper. This was the Lord's Service, as it was called. And therefore, as you know, the service of this church, the worship at this church, is centered in the Eucharist."

He paused. And the tightness in the faces eased. "But it's more than that."

He smiled broadly. "Jesus, in speaking to the woman at the well, said God desires that we worship Him in spirit and in truth."[3]

His eyes scanned the sanctuary. "What does it mean to worship God in spirit?"

Another slight pause. "Well, it doesn't mean to worship Him in a *spirited* way—although I think that that is a part of it. I can't imagine the kind of gloominess that one finds in many churches being in any way an honor and glory to almighty God—especially if you read the Scriptures and find out that the Lord invites us to *delight* ourselves in Him."[4]

Again, a quick smile. "You know, Episcopalians are rather good in holding God in awe and reverence—and at arm's length. But our God desires to be delighted in, to be rejoiced in,[5] to be loved and worshiped in that way."

Immediately, his speech pattern quickened, and intensity filled the room. It was not heavy, however; it was light and cheerful. In many hours of searching, I

---

[3]John 4:23.   [4]Psalm 37:4.   [5]Philippians 4:4.

found no explanation for this phenomenon in the church except that an intensity, a sort of pleasant electricity, seemed to manifest itself at certain key moments in Fullam's teaching. After it passed, I wasn't always absolutely sure it had occurred. And yet I knew it had. Terry lifted his Bible from the lectern and spoke on:

But what does it mean, to worship in spirit? St. Paul tells us in Romans 12:1: "I beseech you therefore, brethren, by the mercies of God, that you present your bodies a living sacrifice, holy and acceptable to God, which is your spiritual worship."[6]

I've told you so many times, it almost embarrasses me to repeat it, that worship is not going through the liturgy, however lovely. Worship is not the singing of hymns or the reading of prayers. *Worship is the offering of your own life to the Lord in response to Him.* Without that, you have not worshiped.

It's very clear in the New Testament. Jesus said to the woman, "for God seeks such to worship him."[7] Concerning the Pharisees, in Matthew 15, the Lord said that those people did not worship God—"in vain do they worship me."[8] There is a kind of worship that is not acceptable to God—that kind of repetitious worship that is nothing more than words and ceremonies.

If you come to this place and stand and sing the hymns that are announced, if you read the prayers that are set before you, if you listen to the sermon, and even if you receive the sacrament, *if you all the time are withholding your own life from the Lord, don't think for one moment that you've worshiped God.* Worship involves the giving of ourselves to the Lord.

That's why no one can worship for me. I can be in

---

[6]Here, as was so often the case, he was not actually quoting from the Bible in front of him, but was mixing King James with RSV from memory.

[7]John 4:23.   [8]Matthew 15:9, quoting Isaiah.

the midst of a worshiping crowd and yet be an island of resistance—because God does not regard the outward appearance. It would be possible for me to kneel, to raise my hands, and to make the sign of the cross, and no one around knows the depths of my heart, whether it is far from the Lord or not. But we know. And God knows.

That's why we begin our services reminding ourselves of the God with whom we have to do: "Almighty God, unto whom all hearts are open, all desires known, and *from whom no secrets are hid.*"[9]

Unafraid of Practice

Fullam had been at St. Paul's for several months when I attended my first Wednesday night Bible study there. Attendance at the meetings had multiplied rapidly in just a few weeks from an initial group of fifty to more than two hundred my first night. And the increase continued rapidly, mounting to four hundred and more some nights and finally spilling over from the low-ceilinged parish hall into the sanctuary, where closed-circuit television and strong amplifiers were provided. The church even experimented with multiple nights for Bible study and a venture into a neighboring Episcopal church. But most of those experiments were short-lived and the sardine-can conditions were accepted, and enjoyed. People came great distances for the teachings, some from other churches and denominations, some merely dabbling out of curiosity.

Terry was seated at the piano placed in front of the semicircular group when I entered. The meeting had begun. I was impressed with the variety of people and attire. Some were elderly, some very young, most in the young-adult to middle-age range. There was long hair and short hair, bermuda shorts to accommodate the warm

---

[9]Book of Common Prayer.

evening, and business suits reflecting the tight schedules
of men commuting to New York City. And contrary to
many charismatic meetings popular at that time, nearly
50 percent of the group was male.

Phil March was right. Fullam knew how to use music to
break the ice, whether for Bible study or worship. He was
doing it at that moment.

"Now this is an easy one," he was saying, "with a
beautiful melody and simple words. But it's a round. And
it can get difficult if you don't concentrate. But first let's
sing it all together. Some of you have heard it."

His large hands moved over the piano keys. "I'll sing it
first, and you follow me:

Father, I adore you,
Lay my life before you;
How I love you."

He enunciated exaggeratedly, and nodded his head
forcefully at the beginning of each line. His was not a
powerful solo voice, but it was clear and pleasant, with
seemingly perfect pitch.

"Now the second time around," he said, stopping
momentarily, his hands still resting on the keys, "it's
'Jesus, I adore you,' and then the third time 'Spirit, I
adore you.' Do you see?"

His hands moved upon the keys again, his head came
forward, and we all sang. It wasn't bad. We did it a second
time, and it was better, quite good in fact. The low ceiling
seemed to enhance the tone. Terry stopped again.

"Now this time, we'll do it as a round."

He was smiling widely, actually beaming. He loved it.
If he was comfortable in teaching, he was equally so in
music. It had been his life for so long.

"This section here will begin. And then the middle

group here will begin when the first group completes the first part. And then this section over here will come in last. Got it?"

He chuckled. "You have to think, now, and don't worry about what the other group is doing."

We got through the first part okay. And we were showing promise on the second part, but on the third, we fell apart. Terry stopped playing, got up from the piano, and waved his arms.

"Hold it! Whoa!"

He feigned seriousness, but was still beaming. "I thought we were singing to the glory of God! You must be kidding!"

Everyone laughed, but many of us looked a bit sheepish.

"Now let's try it again," he said. "And stick to your part. Sing it beautifully. Really sing it to the glory of God."

We were much better the second time, and the third time we were very good. I sensed that we really were singing to the Lord. With Terry leading the way on the piano, we moved readily from one simple song of worship to another, spending most of the next twenty minutes on several of the new songs that were becoming increasingly popular in the charismatic renewal. But now and then he led us into a traditional hymn, which we sang with the same devotion.

As the last note faded away, Terry prayed briefly for God's blessing and direction for the Bible study. We meant business and were ready to learn.

My first Sunday service under Fullam's ministry also revealed the importance of music in additional aspects of worship. The processional had occurred, we had been welcomed in the name of the Lord, and all two hundred twenty-five of us—maybe two hundred fifty, for it was tight—were settling down for a happy time.

"I have another song for you."

Everyone smiled, and a few chuckled audibly as Terry stood full-robed and spread-armed before us. The remembrance evokes a line by one of the more outgoing parishioners some years later when a visiting minister, Dennis Bennett, commended the church for its singing.

"We sing under duress," remarked Lee Buck from the back of the room. Perhaps "happy coercion" was more accurate.

"It goes like this," Terry said that Sunday morning, moving his right hand in accompaniment, almost as though it held a conductor's baton:

Let all that is within me cry holy!
Let all that is within me cry holy!
Holy! Holy!
Holy is the Lamb that was slain.

We sang well. Indeed, we sang very well. If we hadn't, he would have stopped us, rehearsed us, and had us start over again, which he often did. There were many accomplished singers who were able to provide harmony and a proper rising and falling in volume. We actually worshiped the Lord.

But it was nearly forty-five minutes later when that worship took on an extra dimension. Terry was celebrating Communion, assisted by two lay readers. The people began to file forward to be served and he started to sing *a cappella* the song we had learned earlier. Gradually the choir and then the congregation joined in. This was not an Episcopal custom in that spring of 1973. The singing swelled as verse after verse was added. First it was "Let all that is within me cry *holy*." Then "Let all that is within me cry *worthy*." Then "glory," then "Jesus." The Communion was very sweet.

As the scores continued to file forward, and then return ever so prayerfully, the song shifted to "Alleluia," over and over, verse after verse, "My Redeemer . . . Jesus is Lord . . . If you love Him, why not serve Him? . . . alleluia. . . ."

Many of those Episcopalians—and those Presbyterians, and those Lutherans, and those whatever—had never worshiped in song at that point in the service. They had never lifted their voices or their hands to the Lord in such adoration.

From the middle of the sanctuary, a sweet soprano voice lifted to great, delicate heights, and then blended in with the others. I knew it was Diane Kelley. Once a fine singer, she had stopped, seemingly having lost her voice. But in deep worship, it was there—bell-like, then whispery, holy.

Internal and External

Free worship was difficult for many of the people at St. Paul's, as it was among Episcopalians generally and other sacramental, liturgical groups. And affluence, advanced education, and the urbanity of New York suburban life did not promote freedom of expression in worship either. Patience and understanding were required, along with teaching.

The latter came persistently. The parishioners were led, for example, into an examination of Romans 1:21: "For although they knew God they did not honor him as God or give thanks to him, but they became futile in their thinking and their senseless minds were darkened."

Those the apostle was writing about knew God, but they did not honor Him as God; they did not glorify Him;

they did not give Him the worship that was due Him. Not worshiping the Lord, they did not, as Terry had taught, *give themselves* to Him. They gave Him other things perhaps—their goods, their sacrifices. But they did not give themselves as living sacrifices, which was their *spiritual worship*.

So it seemed that it was not enough to *know about* God, or even to *know* God, if one didn't *worship* God. Eventually, it seemed, there came a drying up, a futility, a darkening, and a collapse.

The drying up, the darkening, was inevitable because, according to Psalm 22:3, God, who is holy, inhabits the praises of Israel, His people—He is "enthroned" on their praises. He lives in the praises, the worship and adoration, of His people; He assumes His proper place, on the throne. Reality is achieved. Without the worship, the components of reality are not in order; God is not seen as on His throne. To our senses, reality evaporates. Darkness threatens.

Undergirding this is an old chestnut in Scripture, part of which is spoken Sunday after Sunday by participants in Episcopal services. It is found in Psalm 51:15-17:

O Lord, open thou my lips,
  and my mouth shall show forth thy praise
For thou hast no delight in sacrifice;
  were I to give a burnt offering, thou wouldst
  not be pleased.
The sacrifice acceptable to God is a broken spirit;
  a broken and contrite heart, O God, thou wilt not
  despise.

In that declaration, we suggest an understanding of our duty to praise and worship God and we acknowledge that the pathway for that praise is through the giving of ourselves, the humbling and breaking of our proud spirits and hearts. We indicate a belief that we must give ourselves fully to the Lord in worship of Him, or it will be as nothing.

The people of St. Paul's ever so gradually found themselves giving themselves inwardly in their worship. They drew closer and closer to the Lord, especially individually. But, as they did so and let the reasons for their worship, as found in Scripture, sink into their hearts, they found themselves giving quiet *external* expression to their worship also.

I recall vividly seeing this overt expression for the first time at St. Paul's, following an absence of several months. I noticed it first during the singing of a simple song that line by line elevated personal and collective worship to the highest form.

> We have come into His house and called upon His
>   name to worship Him;
> We have come into His house and called upon His
>   name to worship Him;
> We have come into His house and called upon His
>   name to worship Christ the Lord;
> Worship Him, worship Christ the Lord.

It proceeded through numerous verses, including one in which the key line was:

> We have come into His house *to lift up holy
>   hands* and worship Him. . . .

Many pairs of hands were already raised toward heaven, but virtually all in the congregation reached upward, yearning, as the song reached that point.

I knew they were by that time well acquainted with the verses in the Bible calling for that expression of worship and yearning, that turning of the face heavenward and reaching with the hands toward the Creator. I knew they had read, in a little-discussed portion of the Scripture called The Lamentations of Jeremiah, of the people of God and their fall to utter ruin. They had read how Jerusalem had fallen to Nebuchadnezzar of Babylon, how the Temple had been destroyed, how glory had turned to tragedy. And they knew in the depths of despair, the people of Israel had been exhorted to turn back to God.

> Let us test and examine our ways,
>   and return to the Lord!
> Let us *lift up our hearts and hands*
>   *to God in heaven.*[10]

In the midst of their degradation and suffering, in the throes of hopeless humiliation, God's people had been told to lift not only their hearts, but also their hands toward Him. They reached toward the Lord internally and externally. They worshiped Him inwardly, and they worshiped Him outwardly.

The people of St. Paul's were being taught that this yielding of self to their God, this worship with the whole being, was for good times as well as bad, for happy circumstances and for unhappy circumstances. If they wanted God to live in their midst, they must enthrone Him upon their praises and their worship. They were to *know* that He was the head of the church and to *glorify* Him as such.

Today's Language

C.S. Lewis contended that our understanding of God could be impeded by language, particularly archaic

---

[10]Lamentations 3:40-41.

language. He felt that our senses and understanding could be so blunted as to cause us to miss the point of teaching and preaching. This was a question that St. Paul's parish came to grips with in the early stages of its renewal.

In an introduction to a volume of J.B. Phillips' translation of the New Testament epistles in 1947, Lewis argued convincingly for modern translations of the Bible. First, he argued against any idea that the language of the Authorized Version, more generally referred to in America as the King James Version, more accurately reflected the kind of Greek that the New Testament books were written in. New Testament Greek, he said, "is a sort of 'basic' Greek; a language without roots in the soil, a utilitarian, commercial and administrative language." There is nothing solemn or ecclesiastical about it.

"Does this shock us?" he asked. "It ought not to, except as the Incarnation itself ought to shock us. The same divine humility which decreed that God should become a baby at a peasant woman's breast, and later an arrested field-preacher in the hands of the Roman police, decreed also that He should be preached in a vulgar, prosaic and unliterary language."

Second, he pointed out that the Authorized Version had ceased to be a clear translation because the meaning of words had changed. "The same antique glamour which has made it (in the superficial sense) so 'beautiful,' so 'sacred,' so 'comforting,' and so 'inspiring,' " he wrote, "has also made it in many places unintelligible."

The English scholar's third argument was more subtle, but especially telling for Anglicans and Episcopalians. "We must sometimes get away from the Authorized Version, if for no other reason, simply *because* it is so beautiful and so solemn," he said. "Beauty exalts, but beauty also lulls. Early associations endear but they also confuse. Through that beautiful solemnity the transporting or horrifying realities of which the Book tells may come to us blunted and disarmed and we may only sigh with tranquil veneration when we ought to be burning with shame or struck dumb with terror or carried out of ourselves by ravishing hopes and adorations."

Terry Fullam fully appreciated these and other arguments for using the language of the times—real language, undegraded—in pursuing the deep things of God. From the beginning, he taught from the Revised Standard Version of the Bible, although he had grown up on the King James Version and was thoroughly comfortable with it. In fact, when quoting from Scripture, he often inadvertently slipped into King James language.

I encountered him in the hallway of the church one day early in his Darien ministry and asked him about his use of the Revised Standard Version. "I used to teach from the King James," he said, speaking over his shoulder as he descended the stairs. "But I found I had to spend so much time explaining the language that I hardly got around to discussing what the text meant. The new translations are just much easier to work with."

Thus, the RSV became the house Bible at St. Paul's, but there was no insistence that the parishioners use it. Fullam did encourage people—particularly newcomers—to use one of the several good modern translations coming onto the market.

Then the people of St. Paul's went a step further. Seeing that the matter of language applied to worship as well as to learning, they chose to adopt the new liturgy of the Episcopal church from the outset. There was none of the quarreling over the new Prayer Book that tore so many other parishes across the land. They consciously chose to conduct their services in contemporary language that caused them to come face to face with the bare-faced meaning of the liturgy and the sacraments. The Word and the Sacrament were the center of their worship, they said, and they determined to go to the heart of them.

"It may not appear so on the surface," Terry said one day sometime later, "but that was one of the most important decisions we made. It really opened things up for us. And since we went along with the new Prayer Book back in the early days, we had no problems in moving right into it at the various stages. There were never any quarrels or problems. It all made sense."

And that appeared to be what the people of St. Paul's were discovering more and more with each passing year: Christianity makes "sense." As one walks farther along the Way, it becomes increasingly reasonable and logical. It works. And language, which should lead to understanding, enhances that discovery.

As Mr. Lewis said: "There is no such thing as translating a book into another language once and for all [whether it be the Bible or a prayer book] for language is a changing thing. If your son is to have clothes it is no good buying him a suit once and for all: he will grow out of it and have to be reclothed."

Language and Prayer

And there was the matter of prayer. Once again, language became central.

It was a Saturday morning. The foliage was turning in the cool, fall air, offering glimpses of rusty color through the large window to the two hundred twenty-five people crowded into the second session of the parish renewal weekend. Fullam stood near the aisle on the floor of the sanctuary, Bible in hand, frequently pacing to one side and then to the other, looking directly and personally into the eyes of the people.

"We have seen that prayer, as the Lord Jesus conceives of it, is the bringing of our whole life—our present needs, our past, and our future—before the fullness of the Lord God, Father, Son, and Holy Spirit."

He stopped at the center aisle. "Then, you see, there is nothing at all that is exempt from significance in prayer. Some people say, 'Well, I only pray about the big things.' No, everything that is a part of our life is worthy of being offered to the Lord: If it be a need, that we may receive whatever that need calls for; if it's something of which we are ashamed, that we might receive forgiveness and cleansing even as He has promised; if it's an opportunity to thank the Lord for the blessings He has given us, that we will do that."

Turning toward the people on his left, a fairly even mixture of men and women, he continued in a conversational vein: "Every once in a while people find it hard to say thank you on the human level. Sometimes I suppose that carries over to our relationship with the Lord. You know, thanksgiving, I suppose, ought to be the easiest kind of prayer because can it be that anybody here cannot think of many things for which you are profoundly thankful? I really believe you must."

His voice was quite soft and very gentle. "And if that's the case, perhaps you say to yourself, 'Well, I pray quietly, I pray silently, and God knows my heart; you said so this morning, and it must be true.' "

He smiled broadly. "It *is* true." He was referring to the prayer spoken at the beginning of their celebration of the Eucharist a few minutes earlier: "Almighty God, to you all hearts are open, all desires known. . . ."

He swung toward the other side, and almost imperceptibly, another of those deep, almost mystical moments fell. It was a time of true earnestness and powerful simplicity—a hushed moment even in the midst of activity. Terry's words were extraordinarily plain, punctuated with bursts of homely humor:

But there is a time for corporate prayer, when we join together—sustain and support each other in our prayer. And I would like to have us take a little while in our session together today to do that. And there's no better place to begin than to thank the Lord. That wonderful psalm says we come into His gates with thanksgiving. Well, the gates are better than standing out in the cold. It's going to take praise to get you into the courts, you understand, but you can at least come into the gates with thanksgiving.[11]

I would like to ask us to think for a moment silently of someone, of two things, for which we are thankful—really very thankful—and then be willing to express it openly. Let's just sit for a moment and turn ourselves unto the Lord in thanksgiving. Think about things for which you are generally thankful, and *in a most simple, little way* say, "Lord, thank you for—" A lot of people find it hard to compose a long prayer on the spur of the moment. Well, don't do that. Just offer a short expression of thanksgiving—*in your own words, just the way you talk.*

And I'd like to ask that you do it out loud. Now there is a little difficulty here in an assembly as large as this, and because of that it won't do for you to whisper, "Lord, thank you for my dear husband" (barely audible). Now you may be grateful for your dear husband, and I'm sure you are, but what I'd like to have you do is speak right out, "Lord, thank you for my husband!" (almost a shout).

It's not that the Lord is hard of hearing, you understand. It's just that some of his saints are. And we saints want to share in your thanksgivings.

Another thing is that you might be embarrassed if you start to speak and someone else starts at the

---

[11]Psalm 100:4.

same time. Don't be. The circuits of heaven are never jammed.

Let's speak unto the Lord just words of thanksgiving and let the Spirit of God—and believe and pray that the Spirit of God will grant this congregation a real spirit of rejoicing and thanksgiving for the good things He has given to us.

There is no better use for the vocal cords that the Lord has given you than to use them in expression of praise and thanksgiving to our God, who gives us all that we have. So then, let us take some time before the Lord—let us recollect the fact that He is here. He *is* here. Let us *in the most natural and in the simplest way*, just as a child, come before Him filled with our thanksgivings. From there, we can move a little bit later into praise and worship, and then on to petition. We will trust that the Holy Spirit will perfect the worship and the praise of this congregation, and that we may go from here with the peace of the Lord upon us.

CHAPTER SEVEN

Unity

So often when we read history, the very nature of writing, the necessity to organize material into comprehensible units, can mislead us into thinking of the history itself as a tidy, well-organized package. And most of life, before it reaches the status of *history*, is not like that at all. It doesn't happen in easily comprehensible units, readily separable and immediately logical. History flows, and it has many currents running at the same time, some slow, some very rapid. Some start up and then seemingly disappear, only to become prominently visible and more fully developed at a later point. Some merge and are never seen individually again.

So it was with the flourishing of life at St. Paul's Church. Many currents and streams moved forward at once. There were few instances of a stream beginning and flowing to completion before another stream was begun. The Christian life consists of the integration of far too many elements, all dependent upon the development of the other, for that to occur.

The principle of Christ's headship over the church consisted of many concurrent streams, as we have already seen. There was worship, liturgy, and prayer, for example. Another was the devastatingly life-changing principle of unity.

It was a cold, crisp evening in October, 1972. The vestry was holding its first meeting since Fullam had become rector. Things moved along rather routinely for several minutes. According to standard Episcopal practice, Terry presided, in the sense of directing the flow of business and keeping things moving along. From the outset, although he was not notably pushy, he was definitely in charge. He was more than a good traffic cop.

At one point, he leaned forward, placed both elbows on the table, and looked first one way down the length of the table, and then the other, staring fleetingly but directly into the eyes of the fourteen vestry members.

"I am *not* the head of this church," he said flatly, tapping his ball-point pen on the table. All those eyes watched him.

"As we read in Ephesians, Christ is the head of the church. What does that mean?"

Again, he looked up and down the table. The fourteen looked at him blankly, puzzled.

"I know many of you are leaders of businesses and other organizations. It is natural for you to think of the church in organizational terms in which I might be thought of as the president, who works with you as advisers. But the church is more of an organism than it is an organization."

He paused momentarily, and then pressed on. "Now we also know that in 1 Corinthians, the Bible says the church is the body of Christ.[1] 'You *are* the body of Christ.' And then it says Jesus is the head of the body. Now there are churches all over this country that are dead because they have lost the vital connection between Christ and His body."

---

[1] 1 Corinthians 12:27.

He stopped for several seconds; one or two coughed and several exhaled audibly as though they'd been holding their breath.

"Let's take a minute and do a little reflecting," Fullam said. "Let's pretend that that's so, I mean, the church really *is* the body and Jesus *is* the head. What does that mean to you?"

Fifteen seconds of silence followed.

"Well," one of the men spoke with a slight smile, "as you say, it means that *you* are not the head—"

Fullam nodded and softly interrupted, "Absolutely right."

"And," the vestryman continued with hardly a pause, "it would also mean the bishop was not the head."

"Indeed, it does mean that." Fullam nodded again.

There were several more quiet seconds.

The rector spoke softly. "Do you think St. Paul's would be any different if Jesus *was*, in fact, head of the church? Do you think decisions would be made with six members of the vestry voting one way, and eight voting in a different direction?"

"No," said another vestryman immediately. "If Jesus were head of the church, there would be more harmony."

Another added quickly, "We would be of one mind on what to do."

Fullam jumped in. "Do you think that a church—over which He was head—would actually be more unified than is usually the case, if the whole church were receiving its directions from one source?"

Four or five heads nodded at once; then two or three more; and then all nodded. Smiles crept onto the faces of most. But those smiles weren't to last.

Fullam immediately asked another question: "Does Jesus have a *will* for the church?"

Five seconds passed.

"Yes," one person said, and then stopped. "But how can we know what His will is?" he added.

"I'm not sure," said Fullam, and he leaned back in his chair, raised his right hand to his mouth and quickly lowered it. "If He has a will—and I think He does—it can't be too difficult for us to discern. But you must dismiss the notion that Christ will tell *me*, and that I'll pass it on. In too many churches the vestry leaves religious decisions in the rector's hands, while they handle money matters. It seems to me that we must make these decisions together."

He paused and moved his left hand to the back of his head, leaning even farther back in the chair. "St. Paul appealed to the Corinthians, you'll recall, that they all agree and that there be no dissensions among them and that they be united in the same judgment.[2] And Jesus himself prayed for future disciples 'that they may all be one'—you remember—'even as thou, Father, art in me, and I in thee, that they also may be in us, so that the world may believe that thou hast sent me.' "[3]

The room was absolutely silent. Fullam leaned forward again and placed his elbows on the table.

"I'll admit," he went on softly, "that churches are not known for their unity."

He stopped and then spoke quickly, "But perhaps that is because unity has never been expected—or worked for."

He waited. More silence.

He went on, "If Paul is not merely a visionary, and Christ *is* head of the church, there can be only one *will* for the church—the Lord's will. It cannot be arrived at democratically either."

Another slight pause, and a smile. "Every church I have ever been a part of in my entire life has governed itself democratically. After all, we're Americans—you

[2] 1Corinthians 1:10.   [3] John 17:21.

114

vote on everything under the sun. That's the way it's done. And I believe in the American way, you understand, because I think 200 million people will probably do less damage than one person with absolute power. So I believe in democracy—in governments."

He smiled widely, and then turned serious. "I've never, ever in my whole life, heard this question raised in reference to the church."

Fullam and the fourteen sat thoughtfully. Then he spoke quietly, but firmly: "I believe that if we are open to each other and to the Holy Spirit, He will lead us in the right direction—with unity. We ought to try to make no decisions until we come to one judgment."

Sometime later Carl Rodemann, who went on to become senior warden, spoke of that first vestry meeting with Fullam.

"The whole idea of moving only in unity was certainly not a natural one for us," he said. "It's totally contrary to our business techniques. It's contrary even to our democratic processes. It sounds dreadfully unwieldy and darn near impossible."

He smiled and thought for a moment.

"I have to admit something I never really told Terry at the time," he continued, "but I've told him since then. When I first heard him talk about this idea, I said to myself: 'This is absurd. It is not natural to expect unity. It is contrary to good business management to wait until there is a unanimous view on everything. It is impossible.' "

He continued to smile. "But I didn't speak up, nor did anyone else. I just thought, 'We'll indulge Terry in his harmless little fantasy for now. There are enough of us here to keep too much damage from being done.' "

The Issue of Submission

Right away, the leaders and more and more of the parishioners of St. Paul's found that two factors were going to be required before they could expect unity to come. Those were *commitment* and *submission*. They finally saw that if they were going to accomplish anything for God, they must be individually committed to the head of the church, Jesus. That was primary. Next, they were going to have to be submitted to one another.

The foundation for the understanding about submission was found in the last part of chapter five of the Letter to the Ephesians.

"You know, in that passage," Fullam said, "where it talks about husbands and wives and so forth, and talks about wives being submitted to their husbands and so on, somehow everybody talks about that passage without reading the first verse first, which applies to everyone: 'Be subject to one another out of reverence for Christ.' "

"That applies to all," he continued, "and whoever talks about husbands and wives and their relationship must see there that there is a prior relationship of submission to one another. This prior relationship consists of a willingness to be taught by each other and a recognition that God is likely to work in our midst through free interchange together. In other words, God does not lead by telling the leader what to do—whether it's the leader of a family or the leader of a group of Christians."

The principle of submission, without the sort of domination that so many charismatic Christian bodies slipped into in the mid-seventies, was not easy to apply to St. Paul's. It ran contrary to human nature. Mistakes were made; egos were bruised. But the principle was embraced.

At Fullam's second meeting with the vestry came additional light on how the Lord expected to lead a church through unity. Although Rodemann and several of the others figured they were merely indulging the new rector, they had taken the first step toward trying to make it work.

"You know," Fullam said when they gathered in the meeting room, "as I look at you, I really can't tell what's going on in your minds—which is probably a very good thing."

He smiled momentarily. "All of us are aware that there's a private reserve in the back of our minds that nobody can get into unless we choose to reveal it, nobody at all. St. Paul uses that very common truth to teach us something profoundly important about God."

He opened his Bible on the table. "Let's look at it—in First Corinthians, chapter two, let's see, verse eleven."

He had passed out Bibles to the rest of them earlier, and they followed him as he read aloud. " 'For what person knows a man's thoughts except the spirit of the man which is in him? So also no one comprehends the thoughts of God except the Spirit of God.' "

He raised his eyes, wrinkling his forehead. "Nobody knows what's going on in the mind of God except the Spirit of God."

He waited half a second and resumed: " 'Now we have received not the spirit of the world, but the Spirit which is from God.' "

He looked up again. "That's the Spirit we have received—'that we might understand. . . .' "

He pushed the book farther onto the table and straightened up. "In other words, you see, the Holy Spirit has been given to us for the express purpose of leading us into a knowledge of what the will of God is. But He won't lead only one person. That's the thing we have to grasp, you see. He's not going to lead just one person in the church and show him what's the right thing to do. His plan is to lead the whole group."

And, they found, this would come only through commitment and submission.

The Birthplace of God's Purpose

Over the weeks and months and years, those relatively inexperienced Christians gradually tested the truth of one of their rector's statements: "Unity is the birthplace of God's purpose." One teaching in particular, at a Wednesday night Bible study, provided a glimpse at the road map they were following:

I could illustrate it in terms of the action of God itself. If one goes back, way back, into Genesis—"Then God said, 'Let us make man in *our* image, after *our* likeness' "4—that is a kind of plural there referring to the unity of the godhead. In the *unity* of the fellowship of the godhead creation was born.

In chapter three, verse twenty-two, the Lord God said, "Behold, the man has become like one of *us*," and there judgment flowed from the *unity* of the godhead—Father, Son, and Spirit together.

Well, that is also true of the church. In Acts, chapter one, we read that the first Christians were *together in harmony*. In chapter one, verse fourteen it says, "All these *with one accord* devoted themselves to prayer, together with the women and Mary the mother of Jesus, and with his brothers." They were *of one accord*, they devoted themselves to prayer, and what happened? Chapter two—"When

---

4Genesis 1:26.

the day of Pentecost had come, they were *all together* in one place"[5]—and the Spirit of God was poured out upon them, and they began to hear for the very first time the call and the charge to really go out into all the world.

They were *together*, they were in fellowship, in *unity*. You can see it in the thirteenth chapter of Acts: "Now in the church at Antioch there were prophets and teachers," and so forth. It says, "While they were worshiping the Lord and fasting, the Holy Spirit said, 'Set apart for me Barnabas and Saul for the work to which I have called them.' "[6] While they were worshiping, while they were *together*, as the people of God in fellowship, *they heard the voice of the Lord*.

Now I have to tell you something. *Disunity in the church will make the Spirit of God flee*. Disunity in the home will do the same thing. You see, *the unity of the bond of peace that exists in the fellowship of God's people is the condition that is necessary before you'll ever hear the voice of the Lord*. It is in the unity, you see, of the fellowship that the purpose of God is discerned. . . . There is no possibility that together we can discern the will and purpose of God unless we walk together in the light with one another.

Now, I have said this before—I'm just speaking from my experience. My whole life—I was born, as I have said so many times, on Wednesday and I was in church the following Sunday. I've been there ever since. All right, so I know something about churches from experience, from years and years of experience. And let me say that one of the most distinguishing features of the Christian church as I have known it is *division—the* most distinguishing feature. . . . And we'd wonder why, when the gospel was preached,

---

[5]Acts 2:1.   [6]Acts 13:1-2.

why didn't something happen? Where was God in all of this?

Well, you see, we were not together in fellowship, and we couldn't hear and discern the purpose of God, because it's only in the unity of the Spirit, as one remains in fellowship with the other, that we can even hear the Lord.

As Cervantes wrote, "The proof of the pudding is in the eating,"[7] and the people of St. Paul's ate as well as they could, at first with baby spoons and then in bigger and bigger gulps. Sometimes they made themselves sick, not on the pudding, but in their manner of eating. They persisted, however. They were hungry.

"What's been astonishing," said Rodemann later, "is that it worked, and, further, perhaps it's the most important thing that I learned in the three years that I was senior warden. It's had a profound effect on me and on my spiritual life and I think on the part of many people in the parish."

How did it work?

"Well," he said, "a practical example: When a matter comes before the vestry, we hear points of view because people are different. They have different backgrounds, different knowledge, different perspectives, and the discussion is lively—and we have articulate and strong-minded people, and we want to try out ideas on each other. But throughout, what we're trying to do is be open to the Lord. And we recognize that He speaks to us through each other."

He broke into a smile and the corners of his eyes wrinkled as he stopped for a second. "Incidentally, we also have learned that God does not tell the rector in all cases and then the rector tells the people. God speaks through many people, and in the process sometimes one of

---

[7]*Don Quixote.*

those people even has a word for the rector."

He returned to his theme. "If we take a vote and it's divided, well, we conclude that we have not sufficiently waited on the Lord to discern His intent. And we may stop for prayer right then and there in the middle of the vestry meeting, or we may discuss it further, or we may table the matter until the following meeting.

"Sometimes agreement comes quickly, sometimes it takes awhile. And that's all right. It's not always easy, and it's not always clear, and there is nothing automatic or magical about it."

The key point, in the opinion of Rodemann and others at the center of the experiment, was that they grew to *expect* unity to come forth as the natural way of the Lord.

There were many examples where the vestry or other committees took a vote to determine the degree of consensus on a given issue only to find one person standing alone on one side, say by a margin of 15 to 1. Then, after putting the issue aside for a week or more, another show of opinion would find all the others having swung to the original one-person's side, with a vote of 0 to 16.

"What does that tell us?" asked Rodemann. "In our process of learning—which is by no means finished yet—we had to learn that diversity is not the enemy of unity. We had to learn that the Lord sometimes speaks His wisdom through a most unlikely member of the group. We had to learn not to give in just to avoid being thought uncooperative, because maybe the Lord was speaking His wisdom through one of us."

Rodemann and the others talked enthusiastically about the freedom they had found in unity, when "no one wins or loses."

"Supposing a vestrywoman comes up with an idea," said Fullam, "and she says, 'I think this is what we should do,' and someone else will say, 'No, I don't think we should do that for this reason,' and so forth. And somebody else will pitch in, and little by little you see created right before your very eyes a unity. And it finally commends itself to everybody. And it seems to be the right thing. And no one is hurt or offended. And we just move forward."

"I don't know whether you've had the experience that I've had on some other vestries," said Rodemann, "where the week before the vestry meeting, the telephone calls went back and forth, and sides were aligned and votes counted, before the meeting took place. You would have thought you were in a session of Congress."

The war in Southeast Asia was over, and many South Vietnamese refugees were fleeing their war-torn land. There was a strong consensus that St. Paul's Church should adopt a Vietnamese family. It was based on genuine compassion. Committees were organized to find housing, clothing, employment, food, and other necessities.

Clark Johnson, a vestryman and a vice president of a major company, opposed the idea.

"I think we are not paying enough attention to the personal needs of people in our own congregation," he explained. "I know of a half-dozen people who have been unemployed a long time. Two divorced women are in desperate straits. And no one in this congregation is helping."

Even in affluent Darien and the surrounding communities, a confused and floundering stock market and an increasingly troubled society could bring serious distress.

The issues facing the church were basic, centering on suffering people. But Americans were con-science-stricken over the Vietnam war, in differing directions, and the arguments in favor of helping the suffering people from Asia were heavy and persuasive. The consensus grew.

The debate became so emotional one night that Johnson was shaken into saying, "I'll go along with you, though I don't agree."

There was a moment of hanging silence. Fullam began to speak quietly and moved forward in his seat. "We are not looking for forced consent, but heartfelt affirmation."

He waited several moments. "Let's put off a decision for now."

The next vestry meeting came, and the matter was debated again. Still there was no total unity.

A special meeting was called, and the tension was tight. But as the people arrived, they learned that the Vietnamese family had moved to another state, much preferring the warmer climate. Suddenly, the disagreement had evaporated.

People began to ask, "What was the Lord trying to tell us?" Didn't He want Christians helping people like the Vietnamese family? Wasn't that a proper work?

"I think I know," said Reg Jones. "He was trying to sensitize us to the needs of our own people. They're not always as readily seen as those on the outside. The needy in our midst are often almost invisible—someone who has been out of work for a year, and is about to lose his house. We have an obligation to help."

Furthermore, a mistake that might have caused unhappiness to the Vietnamese family was avoided.

One result was a step by the St. Paul's people in a direction that was to be more fully realized later—a *unanimous* decision to set up a special cash assistance program capable of making mortgage payments or otherwise meeting the financial needs of parish families.

Fullam was deadly earnest as he reflected on the principle of unity. "I'm terribly jealous of the unity of this congregation because I know that without it the voice of God is silenced in the church."

But, at the time, one could not help thinking: Could such an absolute be sustained in that sophisticated town? Could it survive the swirling, fuzzy philosophies of the twentieth century?

CHAPTER EIGHT

Money

Tocqueville in his *Democracy in America* was undoubtedly too sweeping and probably too harsh when he wrote that he knew of "no country, indeed, where the love of money has taken stronger hold on the affections of men. . . ."[1] But he was close enough to the truth to make it safe to say that, should one desire an estimation of the deep concerns of a man, whether a Connecticut Yankee or a Texan, he should begin to take actions that will separate him from a significant percentage of his wealth. Matters of one's money tend to set the bodily juices flowing quicker than anything. A threat to that money will send those juices into a flood.

The King James Version of the Bible contains 140 references to money, 88 to riches, 27 to wealth, and 13 to possessions. That's a total of 268, enough to suggest some significance in God's dealing with man.

Money has proved very significant in the Darien story.

St. Paul's was like other churches. As it got further from its humble beginnings, its need for money seemed to inch upward relentlessly. It wasn't that the leaders were

---

[1] *Democracy in America.*

lacking in frugality or good management. They were merely caught in the web of things. There is one indisputable fact in American life: Budgets never shrink. Presidents know this; church treasurers know it, too.

Reg Jones and his wife, Judy, joined St. Paul's in 1964 because "it was a good thing to do; it would help me in my business." As a certified public accountant on the rise, Reg drifted quite easily into the church treasurer's job. That was in 1966, and the pledge budget was $27,000. Reg was to remain influential in financial matters at the church over the years, moving up to chairman of the finance commission to run the church's every-member canvass—the Episcopal church's traditional method of raising money. That was in 1968. In 1970, he moved on up to senior warden, the local church's highest lay office. He was at the hub of things. And that was the year St. Paul's fell short $10,000 in meeting its budget.

"We entered into a faith deficit," said Jones with a flicker of a smile, "the first of a number of faith deficits."

In fact, St. Paul's ran deficits in 1970 and 1971, and the outlook for 1972 was not good. The budget continued to rise.

Suddenly it was the beginning of October, time to gear up for the every-member canvass. "We always had it in October," explained Jones, "in time to beat the United Fund."

To set the stage, it's good to look back at the Scripture, as Jones later did, remembering that neither he nor his colleagues had much awareness of the words of St. Paul to the Corinthians in those seemingly ordinary fall days of 1972:

For the word of the cross is folly to those who are perishing, but to us who are being saved it is the power of God. For it is written, "I will destroy the

wisdom of the wise, and the cleverness of the clever I
will thwart." Where is the wise man? Where is the
scribe? Where is the debater of this age? Has not God
made foolish the wisdom of the world?[2]

"Now, our every-member canvass was run by *wise*
people," Jones said, unable to restrain a smirk. "We
planned ahead. We had all the hallmarks of people who
were wise. We had a canvass chairman, usually a man of
substance—black suit, all that, you know. We had a vice
chairman; doesn't every good organization? We had
captains, we had team leaders, we had callers, we had
instruction kits, we trained people, we wrote letters to
the parish."

He took a deep breath. "We were so organized we made
up a tax table. That was very important here; people here
pay a lot of taxes. We showed them how much they could
save by giving more."

Reg Jones is a bright, but easy-going businessman,
often boyish in manner. He speaks slowly, sometimes
very slowly, in a deep voice easily recognizable in a crowd
of several hundred. The "outrageous" sense of humor that
close friends attribute to him began to bubble to the
surface as he described the fund-raisers of the years
preceding 1972.

"We did everything we could. We got well organized,
and we went out and we called on people Sunday
afternoon. We made them sign a card in front of us. Don't
phone ahead—they might close the door. Be sure to get in
there. Talk about the church—don't bring up money too
quick. Give them the big pitch—tell them how important
it is—how much we need the money. When you think
they're ready to sign, tell them to fill it out."

He spoke entertainingly, but one knew there was
sadness deep in his voice. He was not proud of his

---

[2] 1 Corinthians 1:18-20.

recollections.

"We used to watch the football games right here in the parish hall when we got back while we tallied up the results."

He shook his head. "Being businessmen, we looked at the statistics carefully as the results came in. And we learned one very significant thing: All other things being equal, a caller gives more than a callee. The next year we decided to take advantage of that bit of information. We made more callers—one caller for every callee—one on one!"

His head sagged, and he moved it from side to side. His voice softened. "Oh, what a curse that was to us!" His voice rose. "What a curse that was! People dragged in, made to feel embarrassed if they wouldn't serve as a caller."

He shook his head again, but then raised it and a smile broke across his face. "I want to tell you a story about that."

He immediately feigned seriousness. "A fellow was riding in an airplane, looked across the aisle, and there was a beautiful girl. She had a huge diamond on her finger. He was very interested in gems.

"He slid across the aisle and spoke to her, 'I couldn't help noticing your diamond,' he said. 'Tell me—it's so large—is it famous?'

"She said, 'Yes, it's a Klopman diamond.'

"He said, 'A *Klopman* diamond? Can you tell me something about it?'

"She said, 'Yes, it has a curse with it.'

"Now he was really getting excited. He said, 'What's the curse?'

"She said, 'Mr. Klopman.' "

Curse and all, the wise men of St. Paul's were busily laying plans in the usual way for the 1972 fund drive—for the budget year 1973—when the new rector arrived.

"He was kind of quiet the first few days," recalled Jones. "So hard to imagine now, isn't it?"

Fullam was looking and listening. He was troubled inside, but said little for several days. The thoughts churned within him: "What about the commitment to the Lord? With that you've got everything; without it you've got nothing. We're just raising a budget! We have no ally in the Holy Spirit at all unless we're seeking to bring the people to Jesus. . . ."

As the days wore on, he spoke to several of the people: "This fund-raising thing just doesn't seem right."

He was not especially forceful, and there was little response. Finally he called a meeting of the vestry and the leaders of the canvass.

"I want to call off the every-member canvass," he said flatly. "No one should be embarrassed into contributing. Too many churches are interested in getting money any way they can. I don't feel that this is what God wants us to do."

The silence was stony. The people sitting around the room looked straight ahead for a few seconds and then risked glances at one another.

At last Fullam continued, "One of my observations about churches in general is that they're absolutely paralyzed because they pitch the level of their church to the least committed people lest they offend them. So they're not able to move. Now every church has people who *will* move, but the leaders are so afraid of offending *some* that they paralyze *all*. I see this all over the country."

The silence was still heavy. No one spoke it then, but several acknowledged much later that one thought was very near the surface: "What kind of a nut have we got here?"

One of the vestrymen finally spoke, "You will lose thousands of dollars if we do not call on everyone."

Another joined in, "We have everything all set up—cards are all made out—the affluent call on the affluent—"

The objections flowed. Everyone was genuinely worried.

Terry didn't seem to have an alternative in mind. How were they to trust the Lord for this?

The talk continued for several minutes.

"As long as you have the cards already made out," Terry said slowly, "why not, instead of calling on people, why not just send them to them and then on the appointed Sunday, let's have a Covenant Sunday, when people would make a covenant with God to share their blessings? They can bring their cards and place them on the altar."

"That seemed like a very unusual idea," Jones recalled in a masterpiece of understatement. "In spite of the fact that for thousands of years people who loved God, who feared God, had brought gifts to the altar, to us it seemed like a very strange idea."

Eventually the others embraced the plan. "Let's trust the Lord," muttered one.

Finally, all heads seemed to be nodding in agreement.

Then Carol Sutherland suggested they call a twenty-four-hour "prayer vigil" before pledge Sunday.

"That's a good idea," Fullam said.

Word was spread around the parish. The third Sunday in October was to be Covenant Sunday. Pledge cards were mailed out and people were to bring them that day.

Covenant Sunday

Fullam was in the pulpit, and things were proceeding along quite normally. "He had decided to give a sermon on giving," Jones said. "We thought that was very appropriate—until the sermon started."

"God does not want your money unless you are willing to commit your lives to Him," Terry said evenly.

Many who were in the congregation that morning were certain they heard gasps at that point; others said that may have been an exaggeration—but maybe not.

Jones, the man with the outrageous sense of humor, said, "The ushers began to tremble nervously."

"There was a stony silence, as I recall," he added. "I was sitting up in the choir. I looked out over the congregation. Everyone had his pledge card in his hand. They were motionless."

"You can't tip God," Fullam declared, but without a trace of harshness in his voice. "You can't bribe Him. You can't offer Him conscience money."

He stopped momentarily. "You can't strike a bargain with God."

There was a nervous shuffling in the pews, according to Jones. "The fellow next to me," he recollected, "leaned over and asked me, 'How would you like to be on the follow-up team this year?' "

You can't bribe God! "I'm not sure about the others," Jones said, "but the senior warden trembled. I know. I was the senior warden!"

It must be remembered that few of the principles so crucial to the church's development had been dealt with at this point. So Fullam quickly took the people on a tour of key biblical passages, dwelling several minutes in the Book of Isaiah: "What to me is the multitude of your sacrifices? says the Lord; I have had enough of burnt offerings[3] . . . . Bring no more vain offerings[4]. . . . This people draw near with their mouth and honor me with their lips, while their hearts are far from me[5]. . . ."

Then he went to a workhorse verse that was the key to so much of the Darien experience. "And you remember what St. Paul said in the twelfth chapter of Romans—we've talked about it before—'I appeal to you

[3]Isaiah 1:11.   [4]Isaiah 1:13.   [5]Isaiah 29:13.

131

therefore, brethren, by the mercies of God, to present your bodies as a living sacrifice, holy and acceptable to God, which is your spiritual worship.' "

He placed the Bible on the lectern and gazed across the congregation, making eye contact with person after person. "God does not want your money unless you are willing to commit your lives to Him."

He waited a moment. "Have you committed your life to Christ? Have you made a decision in reference to Christ?"

Another slight pause. "If not, today's a good day to do it."

A grin spread across his face for a second, then vanished. "But if you don't want to do it, I just beg you, don't leave one cent for this church—not because there's anything wrong with your money, but because I cannot let you feel that what you're doing is pleasing to God."

There was not a sound in the church, not even a cough. "I am perfectly willing to tie the future of this church financially to the free and spontaneous giving of those who give out of their love for the Lord—and who don't give a penny more than their love would warrant."

Reg Jones, as noted before, a pivotal man in the movement of things at St. Paul's—"a sort of one-man organizational chart," said Carl Rodemann—reflected on the results of that landmark Sunday morning.

"When he said, 'You can't tip God. . . . I don't want you to do this unless you've given your life to God,' well, as I said, there was some nervous shuffling. Several people tore up their pledge cards. And when we counted up the results, we had barely raised as much as the year before, and, keep in mind, we had had increasing budgets every year."

In fact, the pledging was good compared with earlier

years, climbing to $82,000. However, with expenses moving steadily upward, that left a deficit of $11,000 for the next year's budget—another "faith deficit."

"But," said Jones slowly, "I think perhaps more important than what we raised was the experience that people felt in their lives."

Shirley Bushong was a committed Christian, deepening daily in her walk with the Lord. Her husband, Paul, was not committed, but he attended church. Shirley had been praying for several days about their pledge at St. Paul's.

"What do you want us to give, Lord?" she asked time after time.

Finally she arrived at a figure, and it startled her. It was much larger than any they'd given. What would Paul say? She didn't dare to mention it.

On Covenant Sunday, they were having breakfast, and began to talk about their pledge. "What do you think?"—"I don't know."—"What do you think?"—Back and forth.

"Well," Paul finally said, "I've been thinking about it, and this is what I think we should give." He named the exact figure she had arrived at.

"Praise God!" she exclaimed under her breath, and nearly fell off the chair.

Paul filled out the card, and they went to church.

They ended up in the front row, and Shirley was so excited she could hardly contain herself. She praised the Lord over and over to herself.

Then Terry started to preach. Words like "commit" and "tip" and "bribe" began to pour out of his mouth. Paul reached his hand into his pocket, pulled out the card, and quietly and unobtrusively tore it up.

Shirley went from ecstasy to heartbreak. But afterward she described the episode to friends: "You know, I was in tears, but my husband said to me, 'That man is right. *He is right.* I have not committed my life to Christ. And I'm not ready to do it.' "

By that time, she was able to smile. "Do you know, that's the first decision, as far as I know, that my husband has ever made in reference to his relationship with God."

Paul Bushong and many others that morning made decisions in the light of their attitude toward God. They made decisions in reference to where they stood with the Lord—not on the basis of guilt, or prestige, or humanism. They made decisions that cleared the air, and God was able to work in their lives—to wit: Paul was one among many who subsequently committed their lives to Christ.

It was fourteen and a half months later. St. Paul's Church was closing out the year 1973 on a budget that had grown, because of additional staff and outreach, to $103,000. What kind of recklessness was this? What about the faith deficit on the earlier, smaller budget?

But by then, the end of December, amazing things had happened. They were just two hundred dollars short!

Fullam and the vestry gathered in one of the small downstairs classrooms, and the treasurer wrote figures on a blackboard: $103,000 spent; $102,800 received. Everyone was happy that they had come so close.

But Fullam reached into his pocket and took out an envelope, looking toward the treasurer, Bob Cooper. "By the way, Bob, I have a letter here that came the last week in December. It's addressed to you. I didn't open it."

Cooper opened the envelope. It contained a check for $300. He turned to the blackboard and changed the second figure—$103,100.

Farther Out on the Limb

In 1973, the financial leaders pushed the Covenant

Sunday date back into the Advent season—that time in the church calendar looking toward the incarnation of Christ at His birth.

"We weren't worried about beating the United Fund any more," Jones said, "and it seemed like the right time of the year."

Then, they went one step further. They would trust God all the way and leave matters purely between Him and His people. They adopted the "no-name pledge." People would not sign their pledge cards; they'd merely fill in an amount and the treasurer would have some guidance on what to expect in the year. Only the pledger and the Lord would know who was pledging how much.

"Oh, you should have seen the vestry when that idea came up!" Jones said gleefully. "You can imagine the questions: 'How will we follow up the big givers?' 'What if the figures are hard to read? Who do you check with?' 'How about my tax deduction?' Oh, we could come up with a lot of reasons to stop God's work—all kinds of mechanical interventions that we could figure out.

"Our treasurer at the time—I knew him well—we were at a vestry meeting and talking about the unsigned pledges, and he said, 'Knock on wood.' How do you like that? *Knock on wood!* Boy, was he chastised! He never said that again—but once in a while his hand moved."

Much preparation went into the build-up to the no-name concept on that second Covenant Sunday. Fullam preached; the new associate rector, Rennie Scott, preached. The Bible was probed for teachings on giving.

There was Psalm 116:12: "What shall I render to the Lord for all his bounty to me?" That was the question on everyone's mind—"What am I supposed to pledge?" The psalmist seemed to say that it was impossible to render anything to the Lord that would match His gifts.

There was the great prayer of King David in

1 Chronicles 29, regarding the building of the Temple.
Together they carefully explored verses 10-14:

> Therefore David blessed the Lord in the presence
> of all the assembly; and David said: "Blessed art thou,
> O Lord, the God of Israel our father, for ever and
> ever."

The first thing David did as he approached God, the
people of St. Paul's saw, was to praise Him. They had
been working on that. David continued:

> "Thine, O Lord, is the greatness, and the power, and
> the glory, and the victory, and the majesty; for *all*
> that is in the heavens and in the earth is thine."

All. There was little left to say.

> "Thine is the kingdom, O Lord, and thou art
> exalted as head above all. *Both riches and honor
> come from thee.*"

That had to be pondered. "We had some people who
thought they had created their own riches," said Jones.

> "And thou rulest over all. In thy hand are power
> and might; and in thy hand it is to make great and to
> give strength to all. And now we thank thee, our God,
> and praise thy glorious name."

Thanksgiving and praise—continuously. They were
central. That was the relationship. But then, the
clincher—the word for St. Paul's:

> "But who am I, and what is my people, that we

should be able thus to offer willingly? For *all things come from thee, and of thy own have we given thee.*"

Longtime churchgoers among them had been hearing that spoken before the passing of the collection plates for years. But that day many of them began to see for the first time.

It didn't stop there. "Turn to Malachi," said Fullam.

Dozens of heads snapped up. Faces were blank. "Malachi?" asked Jones. "I never heard of it. Where is it?"

Fullam was smiling. "You know—it's the last book in the Old Testament. Find St. Matthew and turn left."

"A *book* of Malachi?" Jones and the others mused. They were still learning the Bible. It was Malachi 3:8-10, an old standby for people of the Christian faith:

Will man rob God? Yet you are robbing me. But you say, "How are we robbing thee?" *In your tithes and offerings.* You are cursed with a curse, for you are robbing me; the whole nation of you. Bring the *full* tithes into the storehouse, that there may be food in my house; and *thereby put me to the test,* says the Lord of hosts, *if I will not open the windows of heaven for you and pour down for you an overflowing blessing.*

"I'll tell you," Jones declared, "that made a big impression on me. *Tithe.* Ten percent."

He smiled. "One of the fellows in the parish said, 'Ten percent of what?' You know, if you take the taxes out first, it's less. How about a few living expenses? Maybe the mortgage?"

But Fullam's young associate, Rennie Scott, taught that it was ten percent of the full harvest—"a tenth of everything," according to the example set by Abraham in his encounter with Melchizedek.[6]

"There was a shaking again," recalled Jones. "These great truths seemed to have an effect on us!"

And the rector did not let that lesson from Malachi go by without additional comment on verse ten. "We recall that in several places in the New Testament we are told not to tempt God, not to bring Him to the test. But I say to you that this is the one place in the entire Bible where the Lord gives us an opportunity to put Him to the test. This is the one place where we are asked to tempt God."

They were stumbling forward on a central principle of God's. It would take awhile, but they were learning that a person could not outgive the Lord.

Finally, a twenty-four-hour prayer vigil was called for the day before Covenant Sunday. To make sure someone was praying around the clock, a schedule was set up for lay readers. They did not get the choicest slots. "I know," said Jones. "I got 1:00 A.M. to 3:00 A.M."

He hesitated. "Can you imagine that—two hours of praying in the middle of the night? I'd never prayed more than five minutes in my life! What was I going to do there? Fortunately somebody had put out a little advice for me, there in the sanctuary. 'If you don't know what to pray for,' it said, 'how about praying for the parish?' That was a nice thought.

"And there was a parish list there, and I went through it, on my knees, and prayed for every family in the parish—some of whom I knew, and some I didn't know—And I'll tell you, later on I met people in the parish for the first time, and I could actually remember that I had prayed for them—What a blessing it was to me."

So how did Covenant Sunday go? Irrepressible, Jones remembered a story that was illustrative:

"One pledge card came in. It was a little hard to read. The treasurer called me. He said, 'You know, I can't

---

[6]Genesis 14:20.

believe it—it says $100 per week. I think the man forgot to put the period in.'

" 'What do you mean?' I asked him.

"He said, 'I think he means $1.00 a week.'

"I said, 'Well, let me ask you something: After that second zero, is there a period?'

"He said, 'Yes, and two more zeroes underlined.'

"I said, 'Why do you question the Lord? It's $100.00! Did he strike out per week and write per year?' "

It is certain that the most important results of this wrestling with the principles of giving had very little to do with money. They were found in the unanimous expressions of the people: "God has blessed me more than I could ever hope for"; "You ought to see what He's doing with my family"; "I've really found my life at last"; "I never thought I could actually give myself fully to the Lord."

But there were remarkable financial results nonetheless. It's just that they weren't primary. Carl Griffin, the head of a major international accounting firm, who has also served as church treasurer, said it simply for everyone: "I look with awe and wonder at what has happened here financially when a church puts Jesus at the head of everything it does."

The figures producing that awe and wonder were these:

—For the budget year 1973, $82,000 was pledged and $103,000 was received.

—For 1974, $117,000 pledged, $156,000 received.

—For 1975, $177,000 pledged, $250,000 received.

—For 1976, $265,000 pledged, $500,000 received.

Something definitely was happening, but could it be that they were only blowing a gigantic, beautiful bubble that must eventually burst, because of their time and their place? Or could it be that the miracle in Darien would go even beyond personal salvation and finances?

CHAPTER NINE

Power

It would help, in trying to fathom one of the main currents flowing through the Darien experience, to examine thoughtfully three excerpts from Fullam's talks to the growing body of believers. They came in times like those I've mentioned before, when a stillness, a certain goldenness, a poignancy, settled on the moment. Everything was very alive, but almost suspended.

In Colossians, the first chapter, we are told that in Christ dwells all the fullness of the godhead bodily.[1] By the mystery of His grace, the church is to be glorious with the fullness of the presence of God. Somehow we are to manifest the life of God within the church, His body.

A lifeless body is not a beautiful thing—even given all the cosmetic effects with which modern undertakers would try to adorn the body to make it as lifelike as possible.

I always feel a little shudder when I visit a funeral home and somebody says to me, "How natural he looks." Not for a minute! A dead body does not look like a live body. There's something grotesque about

[1] Colossians 1:19.

the whole thing—not grotesque about the body, you understand, but the idea that somehow a dead body is to look like a live body—because it's not. There's the difference between night and day—between a dead body and a live one.

There's something grotesque about the church when the church bears no evidence of life within it. It's a body without life, without any evidence of the power of God or of the presence of God, or anything else—and then people try to pretend it's alive. Every once in a while you run into a church like that. There's something terribly wrong somewhere.

It's not up to us to place blame here or there, but I want you to see that the body is to be something filled with all the fullness of God. What this means to me is that we here at St. Paul's, as one body of Christ, are to be filled with the fullness of God. All that God possesses is resident in the people that are sitting within this room—all that He possesses. And the wonderful thing about it is that someone could be sitting in a group like this in Australia, on the other side of the world from here, and they would say the very same thing—and that's also true.

Somehow we have to understand that we are living cells and members of Christ's body—and the *life*, a pulsating life of God's Holy Spirit that energizes us, and makes us alive, is desirous of manifesting himself within us.

We've got to think of ourselves as members one of another. . . .

Christianity is not an individual thing.

Those words came as something of an aside at a Wednesday evening Bible study in the brightly lighted parish hall, as did the following deeply provocative two

142

sentences:

> The fullness of God dwells in Him. If we are His body, is it extravagant to expect that the fullness of God will dwell in us, His body?

And finally, consider this brief declaration, coming in the middle of a teaching on Tuesday morning in the sanctuary preceding a celebration of the Eucharist:

> The church as it has been organized over the centuries in many ways has become organized into structures that are contrary to the plan of God as expressed in the New Testament. And one thing is perfectly clear: God does not bless that which militates against His purpose.
>
> Now I do not believe that the New Testament church was without structure, without form—that all we're talking about is some free-floating fellowship. That's not what I think the New Testament church was like at all. But it is to say that over the centuries traditions have arisen, structures have evolved and have been "sanctified" by constant usage to the point that people sometimes imagine the church to be quite a different organism than is described on the pages of the New Testament.

Once Again, That First Meeting

To find the beginning of this current, it is necessary to return once again to Fullam's first meeting with the church vestry in October, 1972. It was in that meeting, as shown earlier, that the matter of Jesus as the head of the church, His body, was discussed. As that discussion wore on, Terry, having handed each of the members a Bible, asked them to look at 1 Corinthians 12. He read aloud, beginning at verse 12:

> For just as the body is one and has many members, and all the members of the body, though many, are one body, so it is with Christ. For by one Spirit we were all baptized into one body—Jews or Greeks, slaves or free—and all were made to drink of one Spirit.

He looked up from the Bible and said, "We don't join the church, you see. It's not a club. We are joined *to* it by an act of God." No one said anything, and after a moment he read on:

> For the body does not consist of one member but of many. If the foot should say, "Because I am not a hand, I do not belong to the body," that would not make it any less a part of the body. And if the ear should say, "Because I am not an eye, I do not belong to the body," that would not make it any less a part of the body. If the whole body were an eye, where would be the hearing? If the whole body were an ear, where would be the sense of smell? But as it is, God arranged the organs in the body, each one of them, as He chose. If all were a single organ, where would the body be?

Again, he stopped. "Can you imagine what it would be like if everybody were a mouth?" It was a line he was to use many times in the years ahead. Everyone laughed loudly.

He returned to the text:

> As it is, there are many parts, yet one body. The eye cannot say to the hand, "I have no need of you," nor

again the head to the feet, "I have no need of you."

"You see," Fullam said, "the eye doesn't go anywhere that the foot doesn't take him."

On the contrary, the parts of the body which seem to be weaker are indispensable, and those parts of the body which we think less honorable we invest with the greater honor, and our unpresentable parts are treated with greater modesty, which our more presentable parts do not require. But God has so adjusted the body, giving the greater honor to the inferior part, that there may be no discord in the body, but that the members may have the same care for one another. If one member suffers, all suffer together; if one member is honored, all rejoice together.

"Do you see that?" Fullam asked, pushing his eyeglasses back on his nose. "Isn't that remarkable? And listen to this:

Now you are the body of Christ. . . ."

He interrupted himself. "Listen to that: 'You *are* the body of Christ!' " He spoke the word "are" forcefully. "It doesn't say, 'You're *like* the body,' it says, 'you *are* the body!' " He continued reading:

. . . and individually members of it. And God has appointed in the church first apostles, second prophets, third teachers, then workers of miracles, then healers, helpers, administrators, speakers in various kinds of tongues.

He stopped once more, and leaned back in his chair.

"What do you think that means?" he asked finally.

The silence was far shorter than he'd expected.

"People have different functions within the church, but no one is so insignificant that he doesn't have a place of importance in the body," said a man across the room.

Delight showed on Terry's face, but he said nothing.

Another voice came from nearby: "And that means we've got to find a way to help each person discover what part of the body he or she is."

The ice was broken. Fullam leaned close to the table and made his first confession to the people of the vestry. He told them why he had never considered entering the parish ministry until that unexpected call had come from Reg Jones a few months earlier.

"I was afraid I would fall flat on my face," he said softly, smiling. "I knew I was a teacher and I liked academic life. But for me, counseling, for example, is draining. I would rather teach one week than spend a half-hour in counseling. And I am no administrator or financial manager. Yet these are skills expected of rectors."

He then made a statement that was to be paraphrased many times around the church over the next several months: "If St. Paul himself were the rector of this church, to him would not be given all the skills necessary to bring this congregation to maturity, because God has ordained that the ministry of a church, and *to* a church, be a cooperative effort. No man—I don't care how brilliant he may be—is capable of bringing a whole congregation to maturity. It will take the work of all of us."

An Essential Passage

From his Mount Sinai experience onward, Fullam had known in every recess of his being that he was not to be the head of the church at Darien. Things were to be different. He hadn't known all the fine points but he had known the general principles. But steadily he grew in understanding of even the finer points and bit by bit he perceived the path toward the opening of this "new thing."

Farther and farther the truths seeped into him, to a very practical, workaday level:

The church *is* the body of Christ. . . . It actually is! . . . And Christ, by the Spirit, *is* the life of the church; He lives His life through the church. . . . He actually does! . . . It's not theoretical. . . . The church *is* the continuing presence of God on earth. . . . If the church is a body, and a Christian is a member of that body, then, as with parts of the human body, he cannot grow by himself. . . . A Christian cannot grow into maturity apart from the body, which is the church. . . . There is no way to come to maturity apart from the church. . . .

And every Christian has been called by God to minister. . . . Every Christian is a minister. . . . The whole church is to minister. . . . Jesus Christ has committed the ministry to the whole church. . . . And there is no notion of hierarchy in that commission . . . merely different functions. . . .

Central to this developing current in the life of St. Paul's Church was a passage of Scripture that was to be read, and dissected, and gleaned, and memorized until it almost achieved the status of theme song. It was the first half of chapter four of the Letter of Paul to the Ephesians. Indeed the entire letter had unusual significance in the early days of the Darien experience. It was read and discussed, debated and prayed over, week after week at the Wednesday night Bible studies.

But the fourth chapter, through verse sixteen, was the centerpiece of much of God's move upon the parish:

I therefore, a prisoner for the Lord, beg you to lead

a life worthy of the calling to which you have been called, with all lowliness and meekness, with patience, forbearing one another in love, eager to maintain the unity of the Spirit in the bond of peace. There is one body and one Spirit, just as you were called to the one hope that belongs to your call, one Lord, one faith, one baptism, one God and Father of us all, who is above all and through all and in all. But grace was given to each of us according to the measure of Christ's gift. Therefore it is said,

"When he ascended on high he led a host
    of captives,
  and he gave gifts to men."

(In saying, "He ascended," what does it mean but that he had also descended into the lower parts of the earth? He who descended is he who also ascended far above all the heavens, that he might fill all things.) And his gifts were that some should be apostles, some prophets, some evangelists, some pastors and teachers, to equip the saints, for the work of ministry, for building up the body of Christ, until we all attain to the unity of the faith and of knowledge of the Son of God, to mature manhood, to the measure of the stature of the fulness of Christ; so that we may no longer be children, tossed to and fro and carried about with every wind of doctrine, by the cunning of men, by their craftiness in deceitful wiles. Rather, speaking the truth in love, we are to grow up in every way into him who is the head, into Christ, from whom the whole body, joined and knit together by every joint with which it is supplied, when each part is working properly, makes bodily growth and upbuilds itself in love.

No Spectators Allowed

The current gained momentum and eyes were opened

wide to new possibilities. Carl Rodemann, for example, shared his new insights with visitors from other parishes:

"Too many people have an unfortunate and an archaic understanding of hierarchy in the church, that the first string is the clergy, and the second string is the wardens and vestry, and perhaps there's another third string of other chairmen and elders, and then, fourth, there are the spectators who have paid their admission. Their function is to applaud the performers, or to criticize them. And from time to time, a spectator wanders onto the field and astonishes everyone with what he can do. But that's not too often because most of the time, the people sort of agree that the real way to play the game is to let the professionally paid first team do it.

"Now all of this is so fundamentally contrary to the principle that every man and every woman is a minister."

Fullam drove straight at any who would try to be spectators one Sunday morning, concluding his prayer and declaring immediately: "If St. Paul's is a parish under a call of God, you as members of this parish are also under a call of God. . . . God has put His hand upon the people gathered here in His name and called them to a ministry. . . . Somehow people are beginning to sense that God is leading His people on, and that we, as strange as it may seem, are called of God to serve Him in this hour."

And it was in these teachings that he made one of the most compelling and challenging statements of his ministry. It was not even a central point, yet it stuck out then and in tapes and transcripts later. To a concerned follower of Jesus, to one who loves His church, it caused tears to fill the eyes uncontrollably.

It started slowly. "Now I don't happen to believe that the thing that's needed by the church today is more clever programs. I don't even think we need bigger budgets necessarily."

And then the hammer fell: "*What the world is dying to see is a living example of the power of God resting on people.*"

His theme went on, over and over, with widespread scriptural support and colorful examples. He had a point he felt had to be made, and throughout the years his tenacity has held fast. It is central to everything he feels about the church: "Every person is a minister."

There were many ways to say it, and he used a variety. That Sunday morning the Holy Spirit led him into one of those ways.

"It should come as no surprise to any Christian that we are called to serve," he said, having many times laid down studies on the great commission to Christians as recorded at the end of Matthew's Gospel, the words of Christ about His witnesses as found in Acts, and the variations in the epistles to the effect that "we are his workmanship, created in Christ Jesus for good works, which God prepared beforehand, that we should walk in them."[2]

"All Christians are called to serve," he said flatly, opening his eyes wide until his forehead wrinkled. "We take a child at baptism and we pray that the child might remain Christ's faithful soldier and servant unto his life's end.[3] If that be true, then God is calling up His troops today, and you and I are finding ourselves in a warfare, a spiritual warfare, seeking to deliver people from the bonds of sin and darkness, despair and death. And He has called us to do this in His name and *by His power*."

One of Fullam's major emphases at this time centered on trusting God to empower His people, to know that His Spirit was made available, that all Christians received the *gift* of the Holy Spirit, and that furthermore they could be baptized, immersed, saturated in that Spirit, thus being clothed with power from on high.[4]

"Now the thing that is not often clear to people," he

---

[2] Ephesians 2:10.   [3] The Book of Common Prayer (1928), the Ministration of Holy Baptism.   [4] Luke 24:49.

said, "is that with the *call* of God comes the *promise* of God. If we looked at the call alone, and then considered ourselves, we would have to be overwhelmed by our inadequacy to rise to the occasion."

He was thoroughly aware that God so often had chosen, and still chose, those who seemed to be so inadequate. In Darien, for instance, St. Paul's parish had the second most modest facilities in town. God seemed deliberately, in fact, to choose the foolish to confound the mighty, even as St. Paul wrote in 1 Corinthians 1:27.

But, the rector said, "God is teaching us that He can use people like you and me to do a mighty work for Him, a work that cannot be done *by* us, but that can be done *through* us, by the power of God."

I have never, in traveling throughout the land, encountered a man or woman more quietly convinced, more humbly certain that God will equip those whom He calls. It isn't so much that he preaches it and raves about it; he merely goes about his business assuming that the Lord *will* empower His people.

In talking about Ephesians 4:12—"to equip the saints for the work of ministry"—he liked to note that one of the original uses of the word "equip" was in the context of "fitting a sail so as to catch the wind." And, of course, his next sentence was that God, in equipping the saints, was making them ready to catch the breezes of God's Spirit. He was sure that God did this, that He has given us the Spirit, that it is that Spirit which alone comprehends the thoughts of God and thus gives us the mind of Christ,[5] and that the Lord fits us to move forward with the breeze of the Spirit to do His will.

Fullam took the congregation into the Book of Exodus to show them God's call upon Moses, who was told to

[5] 1 Corinthians 2:9-16.

return to Egypt and lead Israel out of bondage and into the land of promise.

"But Moses had some second thoughts when he heard this call," said Terry. "Listen to his response to the call of God: 'Oh, my Lord, I am not eloquent, either heretofore or since thou hast spoken to thy servant; but I am slow of speech and of tongue.'[6]

"Do you notice what Moses did?" he asked. "Immediately upon realizing that there was a call of God upon him he turned in upon himself and considered his own inadequacy. . . . He looked not to the *promise of God* that goes with the call, but rather to himself."

He paused momentarily, then smiled. "And I like the response of the Lord God. He said, 'Moses, who has made man's mouth? Don't worry that you're not eloquent, don't worry that you can't speak persuasively, don't worry that you are slow of speech. I made your mouth, Moses, and if it's going to be important for you to talk in order to fulfill the ministry that I have called you to—well, remember, Moses, I made your mouth.' "

"But," and the smile was gone, "he said, 'Oh, my Lord, send, I pray, some other person.' Moses heard the call, looked in upon himself, saw his own inadequacy, and did not realize that with the call of God comes the promise of provision."

Fullam straightened and looked out over the congregation. "You and I, and this parish, stand at a critical point, having heard the call clearly enunciated, a call that rests not upon me, but upon all the people of God in this place. The danger is that we will look to our inadequacies. Yes, we do have facilities that are very modest indeed. Or we may look to other limitations, this limitation or that limitation, and wonder, 'How, Lord, can we fulfill what you want us to do?' You and I need to avoid that temptation. The call of God is upon us and that

---

[6] Exodus 4:10.

includes the promise to accomplish that task."

He reinforced his argument with a quick look at the beginning of the Book of Jeremiah where the Lord spoke to the young prophet-to-be: "Before I formed you in the womb I knew you, and before you were born I consecrated you; I appointed you a prophet to the nations."

"Tell me," Fullam said, "do you think God knew you before you were born? Were you a surprise to God in some way? I think not. Consider your parents. Before you were born—think of your father and mother—the most they could have wanted was a child, male or female. I daresay they did not have you in mind. It was God who wanted you here—your particular temperament, your particular personality, your combination of abilities and talents, you yourself. It was God who willed you into existence, and He knew you before you were even born."

He slowed, and his voice softened. "Do you believe that God not only knew you but has ordained your life to be in such a direction that it will be a ministry to people? I do."

And then, as with Moses, he showed the people Jeremiah's response: "Ah, Lord God! Behold, I do not know how to speak, for I am only a youth."

"Again, we see," Fullam said, "Jeremiah turns in upon himself. Having heard the call of God resting upon him, he turns in upon himself. 'Oh, Lord, I can't talk very well; I wouldn't make a very good prophet, Lord; I'm too young.'

"I want you to know: with the call of God comes the promise to provide all that is necessary to carry out that call. There is a call upon your life if you're a Christian. If you have committed your life to Jesus Christ, there's a call of God upon your life. You don't have to look upon yourself and say, 'But I'm so inadequate, I can't do this or that.' It matters not what you cannot do. The call of God brings the assurance that God will surely enable you to do whatever

He calls you to do."

The Parable of the Talents

To Fullam, it was important to establish the two-sidedness of the Lord's equipping of His people for ministry. He felt He must avoid pitfalls encountered through the years, and even recently, by well-meaning people who ended up in misunderstanding about the dual, physical and spiritual, nature of man. So many times such people became super-spiritual, with a total neglect of physical matters, or they went the other way and completely left behind the things of the Spirit. Fullam was determined to avoid such extremism, to lead the people into the truth as revealed by Jesus Christ, who was both fully man and fully God.

He was thoroughly convinced that God equipped people in two ways to serve Him: "One by nature, by the talents and abilities He has given us, and secondly by a supernatural anointing of God's Holy Spirit in order to set those talents aflame and afire for God."

A teaching that registered greatly in Darien grew out of the so-called parable of the talents, as recorded in Matthew 25:14-30. The man going on a journey summons his servants and entrusts them with his property. To one he gives five talents (each talent was an amount of money equal to more than fifteen years' wages of a laborer), to another two, and to another one. The first trades with his five and makes five more; the second does similarly and makes two more; the third buries his and makes nothing. When the man returns he is pleased with the first two and says to them, "Well done, good and faithful servant; you have been faithful over a little, I will set you over much; enter into the joy of your master." But the third, who says he was afraid, gets a different response: "You wicked and slothful servant! You ought to have invested my money with the bankers, and at my coming I should have received what was my own with interest. Cast the worthless servant into the outer darkness."

Fullam felt he did no violence to the parable in considering the talent in its contemporary sense, as an inborn ability.

"God is the master," he said. "What He has given to us does not belong to us either, in terms of abilities, talents, opportunities in life, experiences. Everything that has ever happened to us is part of a conditioning process that God allows us to go through to equip us to serve Him. Nothing that you possess—not one thing, even the breath you breathe that maintains life in your body, given to you moment by moment by the Lord God—none of it is your own."

In taking the people through the parable verse by verse, Fullam said, "I want you to notice something: The Lord spoke the same words of commendation to the man who had the five talents and turned them into ten as He did to the man who had the two talents and turned them into four. . . .

"God expects from us only in proportion to what He has given us. Now if you are a one-talented person, don't complain about your lot. Don't think there's nothing you can do. What God expects of us is directly proportional to what He has given us. You need spend no time moaning or groaning about the talent you do not have, wishing that you were this person and could sing with a beautiful voice or that you could teach effectively or that you could speak in a powerful way. Don't spend a moment wishing for something you do not have."

At that point, he became very personal about the St. Paul's congregation, touching on a general and widespread feeling about what God is doing in Darien. The people listened to him thoughtfully, smiling very little:

But now I have to say something to the parish, as well as to you as individuals. It is an observation that has been made by a number of the visiting priests who have come and spent time among us in days past. Many of them have made this observation: "You have in your congregation people of great ability and natural talent. We don't have anything like that in our churches. We may have one or two, but we don't have anywhere near the concentration of people with ability and skills that you have at St. Paul's."

Now I suspect that's true. There is a concentration in this area of people with tremendous skills and abilities. Now, if that is true, and if there is an assembly of God's people in this place, many of whom He has given great talent and great ability and great opportunities, too, then that means that what God expects of this congregation is far more than what He expects of many congregations.

If you are a person with ability, and there's not a lot of modesty among such people usually—that's okay—I want you to think for a moment of your ability, whatever it is. Don't try to deny it. Don't say, "Well, I can't really do that," or "I don't have any ability; there's nothing I can do." That's simply not true. It's a lie. It's an insult to the God who made you. What God expects of you is directly proportional to what He has given you. If God has assembled in this place people of consummate skill and ability in all kinds of areas, that means the weight of God's call upon us is heavier than we might have imagined. . . .

This poor fellow (with the one talent) accomplished nothing with what he had out of fear—he was afraid. There may be some people in this congregation who will accomplish nothing for God because you're afraid. Oh, don't be afraid! Don't you recognize what God has given you? He can empower and equip in such a way as to produce eternal results. Don't be afraid.

This fellow also had a false idea of the character of the master. It doesn't say the master was extracting where he had not sown. It said that the servant only thought so. There may be people among us who have such a distorted vision of God that they accomplish nothing. I want you to see the greatness of God—the glory, the power of our God—that He has equipped us by nature, by talent, to do mighty things for Him. I want you to dare to offer your life unto the Lord so that He might give you the power of His Holy Spirit and turn this congregation into flaming evangelists that will reach around the earth with their influence for Christ.

It was a powerful moment in the life of St. Paul's Church. And Fullam moved forward. He asked the people to do something new. He asked them to close their eyes—"I'm not checking on you," he said—and keep them closed as he talked to them. He spoke easily and clearly. The people did as he asked.

"In the sight of God," he said, "I want you to realize that you have abilities that God has given you, talents that you have. Don't try to hide it. Admit it before God."

Then he moved into something even more unusual. He asked them to put their hands in their laps with the palms up, open and empty, keeping their eyes closed.

"Now close your hands into two tight fists," he said. "Squeeze and hold your hands gripped as in a fist, and realize for a moment that you hold in your hands your own life. You hold in your hands the abilities God has given you, the possessions He has given you."

It was extremely quiet in the church by this time. His voice was the only sound. There was no scraping or coughing, no sounds of movement. He continued evenly; there was no emotion in his voice.

"Now if in some way you sense the call of God upon you and upon this congregation, I'm just going to ask you, with your eyes closed, continually thinking about yourself in relationship to God, to slowly open your fingers and release your life into the hands of God. Don't do it if you have no intention of doing it, only if you are giving your life to the Lord should you do this. Open your fingers and let that be a symbolic gesture of the offering of yourself unto God.

"If the Bible is clear about anything, it's clear about the fact that God wants nothing from us. He does not want our money. He does not want anything from us, if we withhold our lives."

He gave them the opportunity to let their pasts go, and to consecrate or reconsecrate their lives and their talents—their natural gifts—to the Lord, asking Him to anoint those lives and talents with the Holy Spirit. And once again came a rephrasing of that most compelling, poignant challenge:

"I'll tell you, the world has yet to see what God can do with a congregation of people totally committed to himself." The smashed, broken world—a world made up of suffering men, women, and children—was yearning to see, although it didn't know it, a body of people with the power of God resting upon them.

It is impossible to know for certain how many clenched

fists opened to God during that moment, but seemingly hundreds did. The talents of a privileged, gifted people were released from the bondage of self. Every head was bowed as Terry prayed, still unemotional, still moving ahead on simple facts:

Our Father, we are so aware of the inadequacy of ourselves when we face the call of God upon us. And yet, keep us from the sin of Moses, even Jeremiah, in considering ourselves and thereby offering excuses why we cannot accomplish what you have called us to do. Help us to realize, Lord, everyone sitting here, that today is a day of decision. It's a day when we respond in some measure to the call of God upon our lives. We may not have much to offer, but, Lord, we offer you all that we are, all that we ever hope to be, and trust that you will take this offering of our lives and of the life of this parish, *this corporate life together*—that you will bless it, you will sanctify it, that you will anoint it, with the power of your Spirit, so that your word may go forth and that your work may be accomplished to the ends of the earth. And this we pray in thanksgiving in the name of Jesus our Lord. Amen.

A Spiritual Matter, Too

Then there was the other side of the coin. As I've emphasized, Fullam was purposeful in striving for balance in helping the people to see how God equipped individuals and groups to serve Him.

"Now I run into two kinds of people," he said to define the problem. "I find people who do have a clear understanding of their talents, to some degree, and they are willing to use them, but they have no understanding that they must be anointed by God's Holy Spirit in order to accomplish His purpose. Then I find other people who have a grasp on the fact that God wants to pour His Holy Spirit upon us, but they have no appreciation of the fact that their natural abilities count in this in any way. These are the people who say, after they have sung a beautiful piece or something like that, 'It really wasn't me; it was God.' Well, I understand what they mean, but the fact of the matter is that they're not describing it correctly. The truth is, it *was* them, but as God enabled them.

"You see, we must avoid the two extremes. We are not purely spiritualists in the sense of talking about the power of God upon us—that's part of it—but there's also the other part, the natural talents and abilities that God gave us and expects us to use."

Then he directed his talk once again to the specific congregation. "I suspect many of you men thought that you were brought to this town of Darien in pursuit of a higher position in the company where you work, and maybe that is in some aspect part of it, but I don't believe that's the deepest thing. I believe God is assembling a group of people in this place to whom He has given great abilities and responsibilities, and upon them He wishes to pour out His Holy Spirit so that the world may see a parish alive with the power of God."

Fullam used several episodes from the Scripture to develop his theme of natural abilities and supernatural anointing. In Exodus 35, he showed how God instructed Moses on building the tabernacle, the portable temple the people of Israel were to take with them in their journeys through the wilderness. Moses was a great leader, but apparently unskilled in what they were being instructed to do. So the Lord called two people who were skilled in such matters, as described from verse thirty on.

One was Bezalel, of whom Moses said: The Lord "has filled him with the Spirit of God, with ability, with intelligence, with knowledge, and with all craftsmanship, to devise artistic designs, to work in gold and silver and bronze, in cutting stones for setting, and in carving wood, for work in every skilled craft."

Then the second person is introduced: "And he [God] has inspired him [Bezalel] to teach, both him and Oholiab," filling both of them with ability to do every sort of task, including fine work, such as embroidery and weaving. "Bezalel and Oholiab and every able man in whom the Lord has put ability and intelligence to know how to do any work in the construction of the sanctuary shall work in accordance with all that the Lord has commanded," the Scripture added.

"Now that's an important passage, you see," said Fullam, "because God called by name two people to supervise the work of construction of the tabernacle, and He told them that He gave them ability or the skill to do it. There you see the natural talents. I don't think for one moment that these two men had no skill in things artistic. Indeed not. They had talent that they had developed to a high degree. But, in addition to their natural abilities also came the filling of the Holy Spirit that anointed them in such a way that those talents could be used to accomplish the purpose for which God had given them."

The Book of Numbers, chapter eleven, also makes the same point, and once again Moses is at the center. He is having a terrible time leading the people through the wilderness. They are very rebellious, and time and again are ready to go back to Egypt. Eventually the Lord acts, beginning at verse sixteen:

And the Lord said to Moses, "Gather for me seventy men of the elders of Israel, whom you know to be the elders of the people and officers over them; and bring them to the tent of meeting, and let them take their stand there with you. And I will come down and talk with you there; and I will take some of the spirit which is upon you and put it upon them; and they shall bear the burden of the people with you, that you may not bear it yourself alone.

"Now notice," Fullam taught, "the Lord told Moses to go out and select men from among the elders of the people 'whom you know to be elders' and rulers over them. In other words, those seventy weren't just any old seventy people. These were people who had already demonstrated gifts of leadership, gifts of administration. They were already recognized as elders and rulers."

There were other examples among the naturally talented leaders of the Israelites:

Gideon—Judges 6:34: "But the Spirit of the Lord took possession of Gideon. . . ."

Jephthah—Judges 11:29: "Then the Spirit of the Lord came upon Jephthah. . . ."

Samson—Judges 13:25: "And the Spirit of the Lord began to stir him in Mahanehdan. . . ." And again, in Judges 14:6, 14:19, and 15:14: "And the Spirit of the Lord came mightily upon him. . . ."

Saul—1 Samuel 10:10 and 11:6: ". . . and the spirit of God came mightily upon him. . . ."

And, of course, there was the ultimate example, Jesus Christ, spoken of throughout the Old Testament as, among other things, "the anointed servant." Messiah, in Hebrew, means "anointed one"; *Christos*, in Greek, means the same thing. Fullam often spoke of it like this:

When you stand in a few moments and say, in the words of the Nicene Creed, that you believe in Jesus Christ, what you're saying is that you believe that Jesus is the anointed servant. And what was He anointed with? God's Holy Spirit.

Now the Bible declares, and the creeds say, that Jesus was conceived by the Holy Spirit, that He was the second person of the Holy Trinity—God himself in human form—and yet something happened to Him when He went down to the waters of the Jordan to be baptized by John, and came up, and the Spirit of God came upon Him and He became God's anointed servant.

And this is the way we read it, as Peter explains it to Cornelius, in Acts, chapter ten, verse thirty-eight: "[You know] how God anointed Jesus of Nazareth with the Holy Spirit and with power. . . ."

From there Fullam took his listeners easily and logically through an explanation that this experience of Jesus, this anointing with the Holy Spirit and with power, was what the Scripture prescribes for all Christians. If Jesus was Christ, the anointed one, his followers, the Christians, were "little Christs, little anointed ones."

In His last moments with His disciples, as recorded at the end of Luke's Gospel and at the beginning of the Book of Acts, also generally attributed to Luke, Jesus told them that they were witnesses of His death and resurrection and that they were to preach repentance and forgiveness of sins in His name in the days to come. Then He declared: "And behold, I send *the promise of my Father* upon you; but stay in the city, *until you are clothed with power from on high*."[7]

At the beginning of Acts, Jesus speaks again of *the promise of the Father*, but this time instead of using the phrase "clothed with power from on high," he says: ". . . before many days you shall be *baptized with the Holy Spirit*."

The writings would thus seem to equate "the promise of the Father" with being "clothed with power from on

---

[7] Luke 24:49.

high," which in turn is described as being "baptized with the Holy Spirit." So Jesus was telling His disciples: Don't leave Jerusalem to start fulfilling my commission or call until you have been anointed with the Spirit, baptized with the Spirit, clothed with power.

It was also noted that each of the four Gospels quotes John the Baptist as saying that Jesus—"he who is coming after me"—will "baptize you with the Holy Spirit." This baptism was not to be—it could not be—performed by anyone but Jesus. He has never passed that ministry on to anyone else.

And, finally, the word baptize, deriving from the Greek *baptizo*, means to immerse, to cover, to saturate.

Thus, according to Scripture, Jesus told His disciples—His followers, those on whom He had already breathed, saying, "Receive the Holy Spirit"[8]—that they were to have another encounter with the Spirit. They were to be anointed, or immersed, as He had been.

Then, the Scripture says, "you shall receive power when the Holy Spirit has come *upon* you; and you shall be my witnesses in Jerusalem and in all Judea and Samaria and to the end of the earth."

Was this expecting too much for one little Episcopal church settled deep in what many would call the pits of the Northeast? Could those teachings about divine power from thousands of years ago prove meaningful in this sophisticated age?

Fullam felt so. "For too long, we've seen the churches as a collection of individuals rather than a body," he said. "The body is where the life of the Spirit is manifested—In a church, if the Spirit of God is not present, you have a dead church—What we're doing is to allow the Spirit to remold and refashion a whole congregation along the lines

[8] John 20:22.

of the New Testament—The church *is* the body of Christ—"

But "we won't cease to be an Episcopal church," he said. Was this possible?

CHAPTER TEN

A Working Body

JoAnn Irvine, former parish secretary and now rector's assistant, whose roots go back to the early days of St. Paul's Church, was reflective in the quietness of the downstairs office. The question had caused her to pause.

"Yes," she said, "the majority of the parish are baptized in the Spirit. It's taught as the norm."

She waited a moment. "There is tremendous emphasis on lay ministry. Terry gives you confidence. 'Go ahead and try,' he says. So the people come to the Lord, they're baptized in the Spirit, and many of them move right into the ministry."

She smiled and continued, "Printing the bulletin is as important as going out and preaching. The people have accepted that. There's power there."

I left the office to probe into the lay ministry aspect of the Darien story. I thought that this might be the rarest element in it.

Shortly afterward I read one of the prayers given at the close of a teaching on the manifestations of the Spirit. If this lay ministry thing was to work, it would come from the attitude expressed in that prayer by Terry:

Our Father, we remember your words: "to whom much is given, much is required." We thank you for the blessings of life that have come to us as your people, for health and strength, for opportunities of education, the advantages of living in this land, for employment and jobs in which we can exercise creativity, and the abilities you have given us. We would ask, Lord, that you create in us an eager desire to present all of these good things that come from your hand, back to you. And we ask that by your Holy Spirit you will anoint us as your holy people; we ask that by your Holy Spirit you will let us be chosen, anointed servants of the Lord, Christians in the full sense of the word. And for this we will praise you in the name of our Savior, Jesus Christ. Amen.

I talked to Mike McManus, a very practical man who had not been deeply concerned about the things of God until his Darien experience.

"Perhaps the most exciting idea put into practice at St. Paul's," he said, towering over me, with his eyeglasses slipping down his nose, "is the concept that every person is a minister. It transforms the churchgoer's vision of his or her role from being a passive attender at services into being an active minister of God. Over the years, most Christians have come to feel that it is the clergy's job to visit the sick, to counsel the troubled, to teach and preach. That's not the way it is here."

Such thinking owed some of its shape to a series of Saturday morning meetings that Fullam initiated shortly after his arrival. They coincided for a while with the training of several people as lay readers, a ministry of reading selections of Scripture at the regular services and also assisting in serving the communicants from the chalice during Holy Communion.

"Those meetings were very important," Fullam said later. "What I did was skim off the leadership, or people I thought would be leaders—but not all of them were leaders in those days—and I worked with them for weeks and weeks on Saturday mornings. That would go on for eight or ten months, and I did two cycles like that. It was the concept that Jesus seemed to use. He took a small group of people out of the larger group he ministered to, and spent time with them, invested time with them, talked, shared with them, and so forth. That's what we did."

And, of course, it was a concept that the apostle Paul advocated, and apparently used extensively. It was discipleship in its pure meaning. It is interesting that in the four Gospels the word "apostle" is used relatively little. The twelve are more often referred to as "disciples," which means "learners." When they were with Jesus they were learners. Later, in Acts and the epistles, they were apostles, which means "sent-out ones" or "ambassadors." The apostles, such as Paul, apparently always had learners or disciples with them, such as Timothy and Mark. Those learners went on to become apostles, prophets, evangelists, and the like. However, in terms of their relationship to Jesus, the apostles, even the twelve, always remained learners or disciples.

The First Meetings

It was eight o'clock Saturday morning in the spring of 1973. Arriving with my wife in the sparkling sunshine at the door of the well-scrubbed church complex, a bit weary from a late hour at *The New York Times* the night before, I sat in on one of the Saturday meetings.

Seventeen of us gathered around the piano in the so-called Fellowship Room, which is a bit modest for that designation, and sang four stanzas of a little-known song that has escaped from my memory. We prayed briefly and then dove into a light breakfast of orange juice, pastry, and coffee, with considerable horseplay and good humor. Men outnumbered women about three to one, although the ratio evened out in the months ahead.

Terry, wearing a gray tweed jacket over his black shirt and priest's collar, spoke briefly about the body of Christ and the call upon Christians to minister. I have no certain recollection of the exact Scripture verses he spoke from, but his theme was that the Lord would raise up the ministers within the body at St. Paul's and that the individuals and the body would together perceive ministries that were being established.

"It's not a matter of my going around and tapping people on the shoulder," he said, a point he would emphasize often, right up to the present day.

Many questions were asked, and many opinions given, during the session. Ed Leaton, who would become one of the strong leaders, commented on the number of people that could already be seen doing informal ministries around the parish. Phil March expressed a desire to see more gifts of the Spirit in operation throughout the church and also more personal ministry.

After about two hours, the lay reader candidates assembled to pursue their training and several of us met in small groups to talk and pray.

It was not long before attendance at the Saturday meetings swelled to a size making a move into the larger parish hall necessary. There were frequently seventy or eighty people present, all bent on seeking God's will for themselves in the body of Christ. Word of the meetings spread mostly through ordinary conversation, although they were listed in the weekly calendar. At first, Terry approached the people he suspected were being raised up as leaders and, without any hard sell that might interfere with the Lord's intentions, told them about "the little get-togethers, the teachings and sharings we're having on Saturday mornings."

It was important that there was nothing secretive about the Saturday meetings. They were not exclusive and they were well publicized throughout the parish. A regularly heard declaration at the church was that "all meetings at St. Paul's are open to all members of the parish, and all are invited to attend as many as they desire." It was quickly added, however, that with so many meetings occurring at all levels throughout the parish, it would almost certainly be a mistake for a person to try to attend them all. Such a person would find little time for anything else, for even in the early days dozens of meetings were being held weekly. The advice offered from the pulpit was: "Attend those things you feel the Lord leading you to, the things you are interested in. Not everything is for everyone."

Reflecting on those weeks several years later, Terry said, "The thing that was important there was, it was a basic recycling of the shepherds. Those who were the shepherds, the leaders, were reproducing themselves. It was part of that gaining of the committed and doing something with them, taking those the Lord had identified as ready to move."

He recalled that this was a concept the Lord had spoken to him clearly about at Mount Sinai, to be ready to move ahead with those given to him. "I just came to it on the basis of the word that I was to work with those that the Lord gave me, and that meant those who were ready to move. I wasn't to worry one bit about those who weren't."

He stared at his hands a moment and continued, "I think it's a remnant concept, to tell you the truth. It's the whole idea of the remnant. God always has His faithful remnant. And what you do is work with that remnant. I mean, those are the people who have a heart for God, so you work with them. Never mind how small it is, and the Lord will add to it, those whom He awakens."

He paused another moment. "And what happened is, that core that I began to nurture, teach, and learn to pray with, and all that kind of thing—the Lord added people to them in terms of commitment. They didn't all become leaders, of course, until that group really expanded to be the whole church, but it all began there. And to me, that's a basic consideration if you're going into a church. Identify, help those who are really ready to move, those who will come, those who want to. Don't pitch the life of your church to the least committed people of all. You can't worry about offending people—friends, say, or someone who might send a big check in. Pitch your church to the committed."

Gifts to the Church

As for the concept that "every person is a minister," examination was taking place on all levels. It was a theme heard frequently in Sunday services, at the Saturday meetings, at Wednesday night Bible studies, at Tuesday morning Communion services, and in conversations among two or more people. And generally, the passage from the Letter to the Ephesians, chapter four, quoted in full in the previous chapter, provided the framework for the theme. The importance of this entire letter to St. Paul's Church cannot be overstated. The intense study of it in the early part of Fullam's ministry there provided insights and foundations for much that would come later in the body of Christ life.

One major insight, for example, came from verse ten in chapter two: "For we are his workmanship, created in Christ Jesus for good works, which God prepared beforehand, that we should walk in them."

It was plain that the Lord had a plan for His people, that He prepared them as His workmanship. Everything that occurred was part of that workmanship. And they were to seek His will so as to walk in those good works that He had prepared just for them. It was important for them to see that this was not restrictive. They were *all* His workmanship. *All* had good works they were to walk in. And together, walking in those good works, they were the church, through which the manifold wisdom of God was to be made known.[1] Individually they were members of the household of God,[2] and collectively they were becoming a holy temple, "a dwelling place of God in the Spirit."[3]

But it was in chapter four that they found how this would work. Verse seven told them that "grace was given to *each of us* according to the measure of Christ's gift." Christ was the giver of the grace in which *each* of them walked—the change of heart and the outworking of this in life. They had not earned it, and they had no grounds for complaint.

They read further: "Therefore it is said, 'When he ascended on high he led a host of captives, and *he gave gifts to men'. . . . And his gifts were that some should be apostles, some prophets, some evangelists, some pastors and teachers. . . .*" This seemed to say that the gifts of Christ to men, to the church, were apostles, prophets, and so forth. The ministries were the gifts. For example, an apostle was a gift to the church. That would explain why St. Paul could write in 1 Corinthians 3:21-22: "For all things are yours, whether Paul or Apollos or Cephas. . . ." Paul and Apollos and Cephas (Peter) were Christ's gifts to the church.

Ephesians four pressed on, saying that Christ had given the apostles, prophets, evangelists, pastors and teachers *"to equip the saints for the work of*

---

[1]Ephesians 3:10.   [2]Ephesians 2:19.   [3]Ephesians 2:21-22.

ministry, for building up the body of Christ." The special offices of ministry, in other words, had been given for the purpose of equipping the saints—the Christians, the members of the body—so that *they* could do the work of ministry. And that ministry was the building up of the body of Christ. Thus it was clear that the building up of the church depended not on the clergy but on all the members of the church, the saints.

When confronted with the question, "And who are the saints?" the people at a small meeting at St. Paul's responded eagerly: "That's us!"

They had grasped the key. God raises up some people within the church and gives them special ministries. They are Christ's gift. Their purpose is to equip the saints, the whole church, to go out into the world and minister, to build up the body of Christ. The church was to reproduce itself.

It seemed obvious at last. Most of the Christians would be spending their time ministering *outside* the church, to the world. Only a minority would have a ministry *to* the church.

A favorite saying at St. Paul's through all this was that, "in a sense, the church exists primarily for those who are not yet part of it."

What Is an Apostle?

"The gifts that Christ gives to the church are not mere trinkets." With that, Fullam devoted many consecutive teaching sessions to taking the people through a microscopic examination of the ministries set down by Paul in Ephesians 4:11. He taught, clarified, and exhorted, and because it was themselves that he was talking about, he led the people into the discussion and exploration. They helped to uncover the truth themselves.

What is an apostle?

First, they determined, he is one sent out. And in a sense, all Christians are sent out, so they all have something of an apostolic function. But the apostolic office is more specific than that. Perhaps the best light was cast in the account, in chapter six in the Book of Acts, of the selection of seven men to serve tables and take care of the "daily distribution," an action many describe as the institution of the office of deacon.

By reading between the lines, so to speak, they found a description of the apostles' role. Verse two says, for example: "And the twelve summoned the body of the disciples and said, 'It is not right that we should give up *preaching the word of God* to serve tables.' " And then verse four says: " 'We will devote ourselves to *prayer* and to *the ministry of the word.*' "

It seemed clear then that a major function of the apostles had to do with the Word of God, its preaching and ministry. And what did that mean?

An examination of the sort of thing the apostles proclaimed, as recorded in Acts, made it plain that this preaching and ministry consisted of setting forth the great redemptive facts upon which the Christian faith rests. Peter's preaching on two occasions, as described in the second and third chapters, was illustrative: Jesus, as foretold in the Old Testament, was sent, crucified, and resurrected; He ascended, was exalted, and poured out the Holy Spirit, among other things.

Although most of the ministry found in the Book of Acts seems to take the form of preaching—with the design of bringing people to a decision—it is obvious that the apostles also taught, with the aim of instructing those who had made a decision for Christ. The phrase "ministry of the word" certainly seems to include not only a compelling sort of preaching, but also teaching and the guarding of the truth. Further understanding on this was found in Acts 2:41-42: "So those who received his [Peter's] word were baptized, and there were added that day about three thousand souls. And they devoted themselves to the *apostles' teaching and fellowship, to the breaking of bread and the prayers.*"

The observance of the Lord's Supper was a central part of the early church's worship services, often coinciding with the sharing of a meal by the fellowship, but it was not celebrated without the simultaneous ministry of the word. The word and the sacrament went together, for without the word, without the foundation and understanding that it offered, the sacrament observed by itself over any substantial period inevitably entered into trouble. Superstition and abuse arose. The apostle Paul had to deal with such problems in the First Letter to the Corinthians, chapter eleven.

On the other hand, the Word without the sacrament tended to enter into lifelessness and flatness that the celebration of the Eucharist overcame.

Thus, it seemed, the apostles' function of prayer and the ministry of the Word served to guard and stabilize the worship services. However, since little of this ministry was localized because of the wide travel of the apostles, these functions were eventually passed on to others on the local level, as was to become clear in the continuing studies at Darien.

It was also seen, especially in going beyond the first twelve, that the office of apostle, while one of authority, was just one among several offices. There was little notion, if any, of hierarchy. The apostle had his function, which was mostly trans-local, and the prophet or the pastor had his. They were not exactly equal, but they did not "lord" it over one another either, for they remembered the words of Jesus: "You know that the rulers of the Gentiles lord it over them, and their great men exercise authority over them. It shall not be so among you. . . ."[4]

As Fullam explained to the people of St. Paul's: "None of this has a thing to do with ordination. Man cannot make ministries, according to the New Testament. Ordination is merely recognition of a ministry already given by God."

What Is a Prophet?

Next came the question: What is a prophet?

"Prophecy is of supreme importance," declared Fullam. "The church without the living voice of prophecy is missing the blessing of God."

To support this, he took the people to the beginning of chapter fourteen of First Corinthians.

"Look at what Paul says," he began, holding his Bible in front of him, " 'Make love your aim, and *earnestly desire* the spiritual gifts, *especially that you may prophesy.*' "

He looked up from his Bible. "Do you see that? He urges the people to *seek* the manifestations of the Spirit. There's nothing half-hearted about it. He *especially* wants them to prophesy. It's important. If you look at verse three, you'll see why. Look at what it says: '. . . he who prophesies speaks to men for their upbuilding and encouragement and consolation.' "

He tucked the Bible under his arm and took one step to the right. "Do you see what prophecy does? It builds up, it encourages, it consoles. It is constructive."

He paused a moment, head slightly lowered, and continued: "Something is wrong when this doesn't happen. Something is wrong when a word from the Lord produces heaviness or bondage. It should produce a lightness, a removing of burdens. Oh, it may be a strong word, and you may not like it for a minute or two, but it should produce a lightness, a relief, encouragement and

[4]Matthew 20:25-26.

consolation."

Looking into the faces of several people in the front pews and then back out over the congregation, he said rather softly, "God can take a word and reach into the heart of a person—cutting through years of debris and setting that person free. He would like to have eight hundred people in St. Paul's who could manifest prophecy when it is needed."

Fullam explained that the New Testament teaches all Christians may prophesy as the Holy Spirit wills, depending upon the need of the moment. But, he said, not all Christians are called to be prophets; not all are called to that ministry. It has a special function.

In that special sense, viewing it as an office, several passages of Scripture shed light, some already touched on in teachings on other subjects. In Exodus 4, there is the dialogue after God tells Moses He will equip him for leading the people of Israel out of Egypt. Moses cowers, says he's not eloquent and so on. The Lord becomes exasperated and says, in effect, "Okay, Moses, I'll use your brother Aaron." In verse 16, God adds that Aaron "shall speak for you to the people; and he shall be a *mouth* for you, and you shall be to him as God." Further on, in verse one of chapter seven, God says of the Moses-Aaron relationship, "Aaron your brother shall be your prophet."

So they saw the Scripture likening Moses to God and likening Aaron to a "prophet" or a "mouth"; a prophet was like a mouth. Thus a prophet of God is a mouth or mouthpiece for God.

"You can see," said Fullam, "a prophet is one who speaks, or delivers, the word of the Lord."

In quick order, he took them into the twenty-third chapter of Jeremiah, which had been important to him prior to his Mount Sinai experience in 1972. There the congregation received a good understanding of what a true prophet is by reading a description of a false prophet. The whole chapter addresses the point, but verse sixteen says plainly that false prophets speak their own words, "visions of their own minds, not from the mouth of the Lord." The true prophet, then, obviously speaks the words from the mouth of the Lord, as he is told. He is the mouthpiece.

Verse 17 goes on to say that the effect of false prophecy is to cause the people to follow their own heart, ignoring the leading and will of the Lord. "No evil shall come upon you," the false prophet says, and then disaster inevitably results.

But, following through from there, the true prophet "has stood in the council of the Lord to perceive and to hear his word. . . . If they had stood in my council, then they would have proclaimed my words to my people."

And the effect of the true prophecy, as found in the second half of verse twenty-two, is just the opposite of that from the false prophet. It turns the people "from their evil way, and from the evil of their doings." The false prophet, in other words, causes disobedience; the true prophet leads the people to obedience—from storm and wrath to peace and prosperity.

"It is more important for people to hear the word of God," declared Fullam, "than anything else. It is not mere human advice. And it is not always introduced by some stentorian proclamation of 'thus saith the Lord' or 'the word of the Lord came unto me today.' It is merely speaking the words of the Lord into a situation, quietly and humbly."

He looked out over the gathering of people and asked a haunting question: "What would happen to the area around us if living, healing waters were flowing regularly from here?"

He paused and answered his own question: "People

would come from everywhere."

A Study of the Evangelist
What is an evangelist?

The word is used only three times in the Bible. One comes in the Ephesians four passage. Another is in Acts 21:8, where Luke tells of going with Paul to the house of Philip the evangelist. This is presumably the same Philip described in Acts as going to Samaria and proclaiming the word, casting out unclean spirits and healing the paralyzed and lame.[5] He also was the one who encountered the Ethiopian eunuch. He "opened his mouth, and beginning with this scripture *he told him the good news of Jesus*," later baptizing him.[6]

The third reference to evangelist comes in Paul's Second Letter to Timothy: "As for you, always be steady, endure suffering, *do the work of an evangelist*, fulfill your ministry."[7]

Growing from the same word roots, "gospel" *(evangelion)* is the message of the good news and "evangelist" is the one who proclaims that message.

It was helpful to the Darien study when, not long ago, the Episcopal church found in a survey that the activity its members felt was most needed was evangelism. Not noted for their attention to this work, the church leaders decided the best thing to do was appoint a commission to determine what it really meant. What was evangelism? Happily, that commission, with Fullam as a member, came up with this definition:

"To evangelize is to present Jesus Christ in the power of the Holy Spirit in such a way as to cause people to come to believe in Him as their Savior and to follow Him as Lord in the fellowship of the church."

Apostles and evangelists sounded at first as though they might serve the same function, but there is a

[5]Acts 8:5-7.   [6]Acts 8:27-40.   [7]2 Timothy 4:5.

difference, although there obviously is some overlapping, too.

"An evangelist is essentially a baby doctor," Fullam said. "He brings people, baby Christians, into the church." He proclaims the gospel, always striving to call people into a newer and deeper relationship with God.

Fullam taught the people that an evangelist must operate from several presuppositions, epitomized by St. Paul's teaching in 2 Corinthians 5:16-21:

> From now on therefore, we regard no one from a human point of view; even though we once regarded Christ from a human point of view, we regard him thus no longer. Therefore, if any one is in Christ, he is a new creation; the old has passed away, behold, the new has come. All this is from God, who through Christ reconciled us to himself and *gave us the ministry of reconciliation*; that is, God was in Christ reconciling the world to himself, not counting their trespasses against them, and *entrusting to us the message of reconciliation. So we are ambassadors for Christ*, God making his appeal through us. We beseech you on behalf of Christ, be reconciled to God. For our sake he made him to be sin who knew no sin, so that in him we might become the righteousness of God.

That is what the evangelist must operate from—his message—and that is what he must do with it. He must be deeply burdened with the need for reconciliation between God and man and the knowledge that, God having done His part, there can be no reconciliation until it comes from both parties.

"The reason why churches are drying up all over the world," said Fullam, "is because they have forgotten the message. The evangelist presents that message in a decision-making way. We obviously need more of them. The entire church, to some degree, should be evangelizing, but we also need the specialists."

The Function of Pastor

And what is a pastor?

Fullam's main teaching on this covered several weeks, culminating in a declaration one Tuesday morning that said in essence: There is not a seminary on earth that can create a priest or a pastor. Only God can do it.

Fullam took the people through the Bible to establish that three offices are used virtually interchangeably: (1) presbyter or elder, (2) bishop or overseer, and (3) shepherd or pastor. They denote the same function, and a description of one applies to the others. It was noted that the word "pastor" appears only once in the New Testament, and that is in the Ephesians four passage. In the King James Version, it appears eight times in the Old Testament, all in the Book of Jeremiah, but in more recent translations the word has been rendered "priest" or most often "shepherd."

Looking at elders, the people saw that the word, when describing the office, always appears in the plural in the New Testament. A church did not seem to have one elder; there were always several.

Acts 14:23 says elders were appointed in every church, and little detail is given. But Acts 20:17-28 elaborates. Paul stops at Miletus and calls for the elders at Ephesus to come to him. In that meeting, he sets forth a vivid description of their role:

Take heed to yourselves and *to all the flock, in which the Holy Spirit has made you overseers, to care for the church* of God which he obtained with the blood of his own Son. I know that after my departure fierce wolves will come in among you, not sparing the flock; and from among your own selves will arise men speaking perverse things, to draw away the disciples after them. Therefore *be alert*. . . .

It was clear that the elders were charged with oversight of the whole local church, to care for it, and to protect it. In other places they were called bishops or overseers.

Fullam noted that the word rendered here as "care" is often translated "feed." It was a caring, feeding sort of function, similar in some ways apparently to that of apostles, but pinpointed, distinctly localized.

This similarity to apostles was even more prominent as they examined the Letter to Titus. There it was found—along with a description of the qualities supposed to reside in an elder—that an elder or bishop was to "hold firm to the sure word as taught, so that he may be able to give instruction in sound doctrine and also to confute those who contradict it."[8]

St. Peter gives further insight.[9] First, he addresses the elders as "a fellow elder," which suggests that a sent-out apostle could also be a local elder. Then he exhorts them to "tend the flock of God that is your charge," the word "tend" also bearing the meaning of "feed." He adds that they must do it "not by constraint but willingly, not for shameful gain but eagerly," a clear indication of the attitude expected. And he directs that they must not be "domineering over those in your charge," rather clothing themselves with humility toward one another—a blunt warning to those who would become overbearing or excessively hierarchical.

Once again, Fullam used a negative, rather severe passage of Scripture to make some positive, quite tender

---

[8]Titus 1:9.   [9]1 Peter 5:1-5.

points. It was found in Ezekiel, where the prophet speaks powerfully against the leaders or shepherds of the people of Israel. It showed clearly what God expected of shepherds. Speaking for the Lord, he says:

Should not shepherds *feed* the sheep? You eat the fat, you clothe yourselves with the wool, you slaughter the fatlings; but you do not feed the sheep. *The weak you have not strengthened, the sick you have not healed, the crippled you have not bound up, the strayed you have not brought back, the lost you have not sought, and with force and harshness you have ruled them.*[10]

It is further in this passage that God says He, because of the failure of the leaders, will become "the shepherd of my sheep,"[11] looking ahead to Jesus who was to be the great shepherd. For by turning those negatives into positives, they found a perfect description of the Lord: He *feeds* the sheep, giving himself, the Living Word; He *strengthens the weak*; He *heals the sick*; He *binds up the crippled*; He *brings back the straying*; He *seeks the lost*; He *rules with persuasion and tenderness*. And in that description of the great shepherd lay the description of the shepherd-elder-pastor of His church.

"Doesn't it become clear," asked Fullam, "that, contrary to what we find in most churches, the pastor is to feed, to care for, to tend to the needs of all the people? Isn't it clear that he leads and does not push?"

And, as the rector pointed out, while the leaders do have authority and the people are urged in Scripture to follow them, they bear an awesome and even frightening responsibility as outlined in Hebrews: "Obey your leaders and submit to them; for they are keeping watch over your souls, *as men who will have to give account.*"[12]

---

[10]Ezekiel 34:2-4.   [11]Ezekiel 34:15.   [12]Hebrews 13:17.

"That," he said with a wistful smile, "has given me pause on more than one occasion."

The Teacher

Finally, what is a teacher?

Fullam stood in front of the gathering of disciples on Tuesday morning. The series was drawing to a close.

"All of you teach," he said simply. "Teaching is a pervasive aspect of life; it goes on all the time. But, there is a ministry or office of teaching. There are some with special abilities, special anointing, in this area."

The central characteristic, it seemed, was that a person reached a point where he was able, in a sense, to reproduce himself spiritually in other people. Paul says in 1 Timothy 2:7 that he serves in three capacities—as preacher, apostle, and teacher—a point he restates in 2 Timothy 1:11. But in the former passage, he sheds light on the teaching function, describing himself as "a teacher of the Gentiles *in faith and truth*." Other modern translations render the passage as "a teacher *of the true faith*" and "a teacher *of the faith and the truth*." His teaching led them to the point of faith and into the truth. He reproduced himself in them.

Further understanding on this spiritual reproduction came in Paul's Second Letter to Timothy, whom he has previously addressed as "my true child in the faith" and "my beloved child." He says: ". . . And what you have heard from me before many witnesses entrust to faithful men who will be able to teach others also."[13]

Later he gives an indication of what a teacher is *not* to do: ". . . Charge them before the Lord to avoid disputing about words."[14]

"Avoid controversies that have only to do with words," Fullam interjected. "We have too much of that in some parts of the church today. You can't argue someone into

---

[13] 2 Timothy 2:2.   [14] 2 Timothy 2:14.

the kingdom of God."

On the contrary, he went on, Paul explains at that very point that Timothy is to avoid such things by "rightly handling the word of truth." He restates the point—"have nothing to do with stupid, senseless controversies"—and concludes the exhortation with a revealing description of the proper teaching method and its result: ". . . The Lord's servant must not be quarrelsome but kindly to every one, *an apt teacher, forbearing, correcting his opponents with gentleness.* God may perhaps grant that they will repent and come to know the truth."[15]

"Apt" is a significant word in the passage. The teacher is to be ready, prepared, unusually fitted, keenly intelligent. Furthermore, as has been demonstrated by some through the years, including Fullam himself, an apt teacher should be able to see a complex subject in its simple, fundamental parts and to enable his listeners to see in the same manner.

As with the leaders and elders, the Bible cautions those who would rush in too quickly to become teachers. Fullam held a passage up before the congregation, and the wistful smile returned.

"I have often trembled over this," he said evenly. "Look at James, chapter three, verse one: 'Let not many of you become teachers, my brethren, for you know that we who teach shall be judged with greater strictness.' "

An Unfinished Painting

What did all of this—the weeks and months of teaching in every conceivable forum, the leadership meetings, the examination of church structures—mean to St. Paul's Church in Darien, Connecticut? Could the ancient experiences be applied in a twentieth-century, cosmopolitan setting? Was the Scripture indeed outmoded on these matters? Had the modern church

---

[15] 2 Timothy 2:23-25.

developed as it must?

A clue to the answers was found on the order of worship specially printed for each Sunday morning service and handed out to members of the congregation. I thumbed through it one Sunday morning and then turned back to the beginning, to the place where churches normally list the key staff members.

It started off all right. "Rector: the Rev. Everett L. Fullam." There was the associate rector, the Rev. Rennie Scott (later Joseph Gatto). But then it said, "Pastor: the Rev. Robert O. Weeks." Bob Weeks was one of the priests on the staff. He, not Terry, was listed as pastor. A little further along, it was even more unusual. "Ministers," it said, and then came the words: "The congregation."

Fullam was rector. But he wasn't the pastor. Someone else had been raised up to oversee the ministry of feeding, tending the sheep, binding up the crippled, healing the sick, without harshness and force. Neither was Fullam the only minister. All eight hundred of those sitting in the morning services were labeled for that function.

But before long it was more than that. There was a lot of overlapping and lines were frequently blurred, but the working body was stirring.

Those doing at least some of the work of pastor, along with Father Weeks, approached fifteen. And the leaders weren't satisfied with that number; they were busily working with more on a regular basis.

Led by Fullam, at least nine, perhaps more, could readily be identified in the function of apostle, to some degree, although not often in the role of establishing local churches.

Hundreds were strong on evangelism, with at least three discernible as bona-fide "baby doctors."

Teachers were everywhere, but certainly a dozen

clearly filled the office.

However, in the ministry of prophet, there was a distinct and much lamented weakness. Prophecy was being spoken, but usually sporadically and without maximum effect. Fullam was gravely concerned that much of the shortcoming of the contemporary church was due to the absence of prophecy, and he and others were readily seeking the Lord over this weakness. They were aware of St. Paul's words to the Romans: "Having gifts that differ according to the grace given to us, let us use them: if prophecy, *in proportion to our faith. . . .*" Was faith the problem?

In summary, assessing this refashioning and remolding of old church structures along New Testament lines was a lot like looking at an unfinished painting. I was sure that the painter—the head of the church—saw the finished picture clearly in His mind. But I, looking on, could only discern unperfected elements, often quite beautiful, but still not fully joined together. But I could still get the idea—the work of the ministry was for all the saints, and that ministry was going to build up the church, "until we all attain to the unity of the faith and of the knowledge of the Son of God, to mature manhood, to the measure of the stature of the fulness of Christ."[16]

---

[16]Ephesians 4:13.

CHAPTER ELEVEN

A Loving Fellowship

There is a dream that comes to many people in one form
or another. In one, the dreamer finds himself looking into
the mist and fog, peering, staring, trying to make the eyes
do more, trying to penetrate to what he is certain lies just
behind the veil. If only the mist would clear for one
moment he would see "it"—there just behind the veil. He
strains and stares, unblinking so long that his eyelids
become heavy. He *must* see "it."

In a sense, there was something just beyond view in
Darien. There was an "it" that lay just outside their
experience. "It" was just beyond their steadily maturing
life as the body of Christ under the headship of Jesus, just
beyond their realization of power in the unity of loving and
serving the Lord, just beyond their increasing awareness
of the purpose of ministry. Something was out there in the
fog.

"I have often heard people, as you probably have,"
Fullam said, "people in churches talking about going out
and having a little fellowship in the fellowship room.
Every church has a fellowship room; we're in it right

now."

It was Wednesday night, another time of serious Bible study in the exploding life at St. Paul's Church. Fullam stood before a packed crowd in the parish hall, pacing from side to side occasionally. Another smaller room officially bore the title Fellowship Room, but this large, low room was where much parish activity was carried out.

"What that means, essentially," he went on, "is conversation over coffee or something else, really, most of the time. And the word 'fellowship' has, I think, like so many words, become relatively debased. It can basically mean to most of us today almost any kind of get-together for any sort of purpose."

He paused for a split second. "But I'd like tonight to rescue that word a little bit and put into it some of the meaning that it has, because it has a vastly deeper meaning than conversation over coffee, or even the kind of thing that is likely to happen at a coffee hour after a service."

Pacing slowly toward his right and cutting the air now and then with his right hand, he was the professor once again, standing in front of a classroom. "The word fellowship is a translation of the Greek word *koinonia*, which comes from the word *koinos*, which means 'common' and is the same word Peter used when he said, 'I have never eaten anything that was common or unclean,' meaning anything that was unacceptable to the Mosaic Law. He's talking about food. But, basically, fellowship is 'having things in common'; that's what the word means. *Koinonia*. It means having things in common."

Up came the left hand, holding the Bible, and they were off in pursuit of their theme. None suspected that they were taking the initial steps in a run toward the misty fog, behind which "something" lay.

"I want to begin in First Corinthians, chapter one,

verse nine," he continued, almost gleefully. The sound of
flipping pages sounded for a moment like the ocean
lapping the shore. "And this is what we read: 'God is
faithful, by whom you were called into the fellowship of
his Son, Jesus Christ our Lord.' "

Ensnared in the teacher's habit of emphasis, he
repeated the verse, paused, and then in a few seconds said
it again.

"What were they called into?" he went on. "The church?
No, the church itself is 'the called-out people.' "

He had many times explained that the word church is a
translation of *ekklesia*, which means "called-out ones."
He was saying that the church, which had already been
called out, was being called further—*into fellowship*.

"You are called into the fellowship of His Son, Jesus
Christ our Lord," he said, "and the word 'into' means that
this is the end product of the calling."

The 350 people seated on folding chairs were watching
him and listening, their Bibles opened on their laps. A
quietness gripped the room:

Now the church, you see, the church is people. We
all know that. It's not a building—it's people. The
word "church" refers to people who are responding
together to the Lord—not one person, but a group of
people, the body of Christ. But they are called into
fellowship, so you could say that fellowship is the
end, rather than the means. It's that toward which
everything moves. It's the end of the preaching of the
gospel, as a matter of fact. The preaching of the
gospel is not merely for the saving of souls but to
bring them into a fellowship with Jesus Christ.

Now, I'm interested in the distinction between
ends and means. An end is that toward which
everything moves; it is the final point, for which
things are building up into it. Means, on the other

hand, are those things which are used to achieve some end. Now the thing about fellowship as it's conceived in the Bible—it is not a means, but rather an end. And it is *the* end, I might add, not *an* end. It is *the* end of the preaching of the gospel. We are called by God into a fellowship, into some kind of a comm-union—a communion—where we hold things in common with Jesus Christ.

Now, if you stop and think about that in reference to our other superficial concept of fellowship as mere conviviality, the idea of getting together and kind of having a good time, and so forth—not that there isn't a place for that, you understand—but that certainly isn't the objective of the church, you can be sure. But fellowship as here conceived is the objective of God's calling. You're being called into a fellowship. *All* people are being called into a fellowship, and as you have said so correctly on other occasions, this is the thing the whole world is crying for—a place of belonging, a place of some kind of connection with other people; people feel desperately lonely, and desperately separated and estranged from all sorts of things. And we are being led by God into a fellowship as the end.

Now we have to ask ourselves several questions in connection with that—if that is the end of all Christian enterprise, and it is. Then we should ask ourselves if that which we are doing, as a matter of fact, produces that. I mean, it doesn't make any sense to establish an end and then do something that doesn't lead to it. So there's a sense in which we might ask ourselves with regard to everything we do at St. Paul's—every last thing that we do—does it lead into the fellowship of our Lord Jesus Christ? That means holding things in common with Him.

Does what we do minister to that end? Does it lead people into the fellowship of our Lord Jesus Christ? To stop short of that end is to stop short of what it is God is leading us into.

So you see that any church that does not produce a fellowship of people holding things in common with one another and with the Lord, simply has not achieved the end for which it was founded. You see, fellowship is not something you add on to the rest of church life. It is the ultimate end of it.

The Hard Part Is Ahead

The people obviously glimpsed the principle. Their bright, upturned faces showed understanding to a degree, but they hadn't really penetrated the misty veil. The glimpse of a principle is not always the hardest part in embracing it—as they were to see.

"Now to the sticky part, the hard part," Fullam said, smiling.

With that he took them into one of the Bible's more convoluted passages—beautiful and well-known, but so difficult in syntax as to cause readers to miss some important fine points. It comprises the beginning verses of St. John's First Letter:

That which was from the beginning, which we have heard, which we have seen with our eyes, which we have looked upon and touched with our hands, concerning the word of life—the life was made manifest, and we saw it, and testify to it, and proclaim to you the eternal life which was with the Father and was made manifest to us—that which we have seen and heard we proclaim also to you, so that you may have fellowship with us; and our fellowship is with the Father and with his Son Jesus Christ.

That was only the start, but it laid the foundation. "Why all this proclaiming of the word made flesh," Fullam said, "why all this proclaiming of the gospel, why tell about the love of God and what He has done for us? Well, it says, so that 'you might have fellowship *with us*, and *our fellowship is with the Father and with his Son Jesus Christ.*' "

Once again, it was clear, the purpose—the end—of the preaching of the gospel was fellowship. And that fellowship cut two ways: It was with other Christians, and it was with God. They all together were holding something in common—life.

"Now, moving on in verse five," Fullam continued, "it's going to move us deeper into our understanding of the *nature* of fellowship and its place in the purpose of God: 'This is the message we have heard from him and proclaim to you, that God is light and in him is no darkness at all.' "

He looked up from his Bible and, without pausing, pressed the point, "When we're talking about God, we are talking about a being who is absolutely consistent all the way through. There are no dark spots in the character of God—at all. He is light through and through. James says there is no 'shadow of turning' in Him.[1] He is absolutely consistent all the way through. He is light."

After a short digression on the mystery of light, he raised his Bible and read more: "Verse six, 'If we say we have fellowship with him while we walk in darkness, we lie and do not live according to the truth.'

"God is light," he said again. "We are called into *fellowship with light.*"

The wheels of understanding surged forward at that instant. Christians, all of them, were called into fellowship with light.

Fullam was moving on. ". . .But if we walk in

---

[1] James 1:17.

darkness it is impossible to have fellowship with light—that's what it's saying. You cannot have fellowship with light and walk in darkness."

Several faces in the parish hall brightened. Light and darkness were not coexistent—that was sensible. Where there was darkness, there obviously was no light. Biblical phrases clicked in several minds: "Once you were darkness, but now you are light in the Lord"[2] . . . "When anything is exposed by the light it becomes visible, for anything that becomes visible is light"[3] . . . "In him was life, and the life was the light of men."[4]

Fullam took several steps, still holding his Bible in front of his face. "Moving on—'but if we walk in the light, as he is in the light, we have fellowship with one another, and the blood of Jesus his Son cleanses us from all sin.' "

His pacing stopped and he turned full to the gathering, his left hand holding his Bible tucked part way under his left arm. "Now stop there and think about that for a moment." His right forefinger brushed his mouth. " 'If we walk in the light as he is in the light'—this would mean, would it not, harmonious with the purpose of God? That's what walking in the light would mean. It would be living open with Him.

"God is light," he repeated. "There's no shadow in Him. And the Scripture tells us that 'men loved darkness rather than light, because their deeds were evil.'[5] Why? Because light exposes. And the last place you want to be, if you're not walking in the light, is in the fellowship of God's people—absolutely the last place you'll want to be. And you'll find the first thing that will happen to people—the first thing that will happen to them—if they begin to slip in their relationship to the Lord, is they will begin to separate themselves from the fellowship of God's people. It always happens, you see."

Without raising his Bible, he spoke the verse again. " 'If

[2]Ephesians 5:8.   [3]Ephesians 5:13.   [4]John 1:4.   [5]John 3:19.

we walk in the light as he is in the light, we have fellowship with one another, and the blood of Jesus his Son cleanses us from all sin.' Now I have heard sermons on the last half of that verse—the blood of Christ cleanses us from all sins—but they don't always make clear that it is a conditional statement. It is not automatic."

His voice lowered almost imperceptibly, and became sharply intense: "And I have to say something that may be startling to you—but the blood of Christ does not cleanse in the dark. There is no cleansing unless one is in the light."

He paused. "Now what does it mean to walk in the dark? It means to walk consciously in opposition to what you know to be the right thing. It means to walk in sin and know it."

His voice raised again, and brightened. "Now, all of us sin, you see. That isn't the problem. It's what we do with that problem. As we will see, there is provision made for it. The point is, there is no forgiveness and there is no cleansing that comes until we move out of darkness, you see—out of that little cocoon we weave around ourselves to protect ourselves—into the light. And that means into a situation where we are honest with God and with one another."

Verse eight—"if we say we have no sin, we deceive ourselves, and the truth is not in us"—led Fullam into an examination of the nature of sin found in the Scripture, that which keeps one from fellowship with God and with fellow Christians. The exploration ranged from "missing the mark" to "lawlessness," from "sliding across the line" to "owing a debt."

"If we try to claim that we have no sin—well, we simply lie," he concluded. "That's all there is to it."

But, there was verse nine: "If we confess our sins, he is faithful and just, and will forgive our sins and cleanse us from all unrighteousness."

"Now, here again is a conditional phrase," Fullam said, jabbing the air with his right forefinger. "It is not automatic. Forgiveness is not automatic."

His eyes swept across the room. "Now what does *confess* mean?"

He paused and there was a momentary shuffling of feet. "It means to step out of darkness into the light." He stood perfectly still for several seconds, and there were no sounds.

I want to take you out of the realm of Bible and theology for a moment and talk about it in the realm of husbands and wives. All right?

Essentially, when something happens to disrupt the relationship between husbands and wives, and perhaps you have a feeling of bitterness which you may not express—but it's there—or you may express it in a very vigorous way, either way. Something has happened to the light surrounding the relationship, and you have moved into darkness. And the fact is, until you are ready to move out of the darkness, back into the light—and the word for that is confess, as we've seen, acknowledge, be willing to face it—then there's no possibility of restoration, and it breaks the fellowship. And the way back, you see, is the willingness and the grace, because it's the grace of God to acknowledge when something is wrong and assume whatever repsonsibility you have for it.

I've often thought, in an argument between husband and wife, that the stronger of the two is the person who can say he's sorry first, because it really isn't a matter of placing blame; it's a matter of being willing. No matter what caused it, something has disrupted the relationship, you see.

Now that wouldn't be so important except for the very embarrassing fact that goes on a bit later. It says, remember, that if we say we have fellowship with God and walk in darkness, we lie, and in the second Chapter it says, "He who says he is in the light and hates his brother is in the darkness still."[6] The fact of the matter is—now here's the point, don't miss it—*our horizontal relationships with one another have been made by God to be the test of our vertical relationship with Him.* It is absolutely impossible for you and me to be out of sorts with one another. You can't have it. You see, the relationships between husbands and wives are very important because there's no possibility of either one of you having a relationship with God if you're out of sorts on the horizontal plane.

Fellowship, you see, is something that can only be had in the light—that's what this is saying—and that means the continual willingness to right whatever circumstances have destroyed the fellowship. And the fact is, you do not have a relationship with God as long as you're walking in darkness with one another on the horizontal plane.

Now, that's a terrifying thing to be told, but it's absolutely true. The New Testament says, if you say you love God and hate your brother, it's a lie—it's impossible. You can't love God and hate your brother.

Quite frankly, this is one of the places where I would have amended the whole thing, had I been in charge. I would have made a relationship with God a completely separate thing from a horizontal relationship, you see—no connection whatever—but the Lord didn't do that. You know the great commandments are loving God with our whole heart

---

[6] 1 John 2:9.

and our neighbor as ourselves. I'd been happier with
the first one, quite frankly. I've found it always much
easier to love God than neighbor—always. But the
point is, it's the neighbor who is the test of one's love
of God. . . .

So you see, somehow in our relationships with one
another, as well as in our families, we have to learn
how to resolve problems that come up that break
fellowship.

Now there is a joy in living in light, open with one
another. . . . You know that when we get out of
fellowship on the horizontal plane our tendency is to
harden ourselves in that position. We don't want
either to receive or to offer forgiveness. I mean,
there's something delicious about anger—have you
noticed? And we rather like to indulge it for a while.
But it kills. It really does—in more ways than one.
Jesus said, to be angry with a brother is, in the sight
of God, as murder.[7]

So you see, somehow we need to know that we
have been called into fellowship. That's the whole
name of the game. It really is. Any kind of
relationship with God that stops short of fellowship
just hasn't achieved anything really.

If it doesn't lead into a holy fellowship where
together we are before God and one another in love
and forgiveness and openness—well then, we just
haven't gone very far.

The People Were Moved

The people were beginning to see through the mist.
Yes, there *was* something out there. If they could only get
their hands around it!

Henrietta Ferree, one of the numerous women leaders
at St. Paul's, wrestled with the problem.

[7]Matthew 5:21-22.

"As we began to be a little bit larger," she said, her accent showing despite her many years away from Texas, "we realized that the Lord was saying something to us, because we didn't *know* everyone; we didn't know how to *meet* everyone; we didn't know how to *talk* to everyone."

As with most of the Darieners, she found direction and comfort in the Bible, in this case, in Galatians 6:9-10: "And let us not grow weary in well-doing, for in due season we shall reap, if we do not lose heart. So then, as we have opportunity, let us do good to all men, and especially to those who are of the household of faith."

Henrietta is a small woman—often an utter workhorse—who can go from total seriousness to erupting, downright raucous laughter in a flash. She was quietly serious when she said, "And so that spoke to us—that we needed to be a caring, loving community for those people God sent to us here."

Her forehead wrinkled and her frequently sparkling eyes were very sad as she reflected: "We need to be a living church that can show God's love to each and every one."

How?

She found a clue in Hosea 11:4—a verse she often shared with inquiring visitors:

I led them with cords of compassion,
    with the bands of love,
and I became to them as one
    who eases the yoke on their jaws,
    and I bent down to them and fed them.

Betty March's thoughts also reflected some of the thinking beginning to find utterance. "There is a need for more 'preferring one another,' "[8] she said just above a whisper. "Sometimes it's a case of too much ego." And she

---

[8]Romans 12:10.

moved quickly to include herself in that observation.

The growing concern was clearly described by Carl Rodemann: "Scripture is very clear on this point—that in this first and great commandment the Lord clearly tied together love of God with love of, and service to, our fellow-man. And we feel this applies to our fellow-men to the ends of the earth certainly, but also to members of our own church body. Remember the quotation from Jesus, 'By this all men will know that you are my disciples, if you have love for one another.' "[9]

He was extraordinarily thoughtful as he, always the pragmatist, placed these teachings in the context of today. "I think we all have to be reminded that the church is a hospital—that everyone there, including the clergy incidentally, needs to be healed, sometimes from some deep hurts and sometimes from the bruises and scrapes of the current week.

"I think we need to be reminded that there's a big difference between a church and a club—that in a club people are joined by common interest, but in a church people have made a commitment to God and to each other."

With a smile playing momentarily at the corners of his mouth, he continued, "I think we need to be reminded that the church family will include some people we would not perhaps have necessarily chosen as friends—and some people we might have actively avoided. And learning to love—that is, to show genuine concern for some not-so-loveable people—is a special dimension of God's grace to us."

One person was perhaps more deeply moved by the demands of genuine fellowship—the holding together and sharing intimately the life in and of Christ—than others. He was Gordon Lyle, a quiet man, self-effacing yet

[9] John 13:35.

confident. He is a successful investment counselor, well-educated and intelligent, who with his wife, Connie, underwent a radical experience with the Lord Jesus Christ.

"People come to St. Paul's who feel great need," he said softly. "People have nowhere to belong. When I joined St. Paul's, we were one big family, in which all knew each other. That's impossible with a thousand people coming on Sunday. Those with *great* needs get taken care of. But there are people in the great middle who are the forgotten people, who also need to be loved and nourished."

Lyle, tall and slender, was a determined man, a sort of Eastern Gary Cooper, and he refused to let his discernment of a shortcoming go untended. He was convinced of the need for more intimacy, more personal involvement in the body of Christ, having long ago been persuaded that every person was a minister. He knew from experience that it was possible for Christians to reach right into the pain and suffering of others and bring healing. Furthermore, he had influence to match his determination. As a vestryman and servant of others in a variety of capacities, he was, despite his modesty, already being acknowledged in many quarters as a bonafide elder.

Lyle knew the answer lay in some sort of small-group ministry, but he lacked a formula for execution. So he began brainstorming possibilities with Fullam, who similarly knew that the key to fulfillment of God's purpose would be found in genuine fellowship—koinonia.

They prayed, and they talked. And Lyle presented proposals. They prayed and talked more.

"Gordon would go back and pray and think about it, and come up with a draft," Fullam recalled sometime later, lounging in the spacious living room of his home set down in the woods near the church. "He must have done six or seven major revisions."

That went on for a year or more, and others were consulted. Finally there was a plan. It called for "extended families" throughout the parish

Leaning back into the soft pillows of the couch, Fullam looked back on those days. "The key was leadership," he said. It always is."

So he said, in December of 1976 he took the list of parish families and prayed over it, selecting forty couples. "I felt they met two criteria," he recalled. First, all had given evidence of some spiritual growth, and none were in any leadership postion in the church. Then I wrote a letter inviting them to an evening meeting to consider the possibility of a new ministry. They all came."

The rector laid before the couples the deep conviction of himself and others that St. Paul's was being called forth as a "caring and loving fellowship." This, he explained, seemed almost certainly to necessitate smaller units—"cells"—within the body of Christ there, which would be like "extended families."

The plan called for each of the extended families to have "a sort of shepherd family, a lead family, a couple."

"I want you to consider the possibility of becoming one of these shepherd couples," Fullam concluded. "It may not be for you, and that is all right There will be other ministries. But I want you to do this, even if you've never done it before: Consider this together, as man and wife; pray about it together. Let the Lord show you *together*."

He asked for their replies in early January. Thirty-eight of the forty couples said they believed they should try it.

"I then went to the congregation," Fullam recalled, "and I told them all about it—how we planned to set up extended families of fifteen to twenty people each, a mix, and how these were not to be Bible study groups or things like that. They were to be cells in the body of Christ and were to meet at least once a month, probably sharing a meal.

" 'We're not going to tell you what to do,' I said to them, 'and we're not going to put anybody in something they don't want to be part of.' I made it clear that this required a commitment to one another, at a level that they might not have experienced before."

A total of 361 people signed up—young, old, single, divorced, married.

Then it was back to the leadership problem. From January through July, Fullam met each Monday night with the thirty-eight couples. "We went through everything," he recollected. "Basic discipleship. What does it mean to be a Christian? What is the church? Personal relationships. Families—after all, how can you expect to have an 'extended family' if you don't know what a 'family' is? Healing. Everything."

From there they moved forward, following three principles in setting up the groups: (1) Don't break up any natural connections or relationships that have already been established between people; (2) assign people to families for the most part, rather than let them pick their own willy-nilly, the theory being that "nobody picks his own real family"; and (3) let geography be a major consideration but not the only one, especially if there are other considerations such as history and temperament.

By September they had put together fifteen units, with many of the trained lead couples doubling up. "Actually, some of them were 'overrextended families' at first," Fullam laughed. They weren't evenly divided for a variety of reasons, some indeed growing to thirty-four or thirty-five people, but regardless they were underway.

In three months enough success was evident to warrant consulting the full congregation again. Many had held back and now apparently regretted it. So Terry went before the whole body on a Sunday in January and invited all to join in. Three hundred and forty more people signed up, raising the total to seven hundred and dictating the creation of additional extended families.

As expected, some people, including a few of those trained for leadership, found such activity was not what they wanted at that time, and they dropped out. The total involvement then settled in somewhere between six hundred and seven hundred, moving up and down for transiency and seasonal reasons, and the number of active extended families leveled off at twenty-seven.

Ed Ferree, a longtime member of St. Paul's, whose leadership roots predated even the Saturday morning discipleship meetings, eventually took over coordination of the program, meeting monthly with the leadership couples for instruction, the sharing of ideas, and praying. The training of new lead couples was then done on the job rather than through special sessions like those conducted in the beginning. The new leaders were expected to rise right within the groups, exhibiting the gifts and talents the Lord had prepared them with.

"It has worked far better than anyone had dared hope," Fullam said some months later. "Like anything, of course, some families are more effective than others. There were *some* disappointments, but nothing terribly serious. Some just didn't catch on. Some didn't work out well for a variety of reasons. Some leaders finally decided it wasn't for them, and that sort of thing. But we've made improvements and changes in leadership, and we believe it's a terribly important ministry."

As I listened to him—this big, deceptively sensitive man of God slouching so casually upon the beige couch—I was sharply struck by his optimism and, even more, his patience. Things, such as this extraordinary concept of fellowship, were deeply important to him, almost as important as his own family, his own life. But, as with his family and his life, he was willing to wait, to move in God's time. He refused to worry. "Everything has a fullness of time," he frequently said, and he was patient. He allowed God to work—in his own life and in the lives of others. He knew he couldn't force it. He could only seek the truth, do what seemed right—and trust God. He fully believed Jesus knew what He was talking about when He admonished His disciples, "Let not your hearts be troubled. . . ."

There were others who were not as passive as he about the progress of the extended family program. They, like him, sensed that this might be where God's plan for St. Paul's Church was to be consummated. They were anxious for it to work, and they agonized over imperfections.

"As set up," one hard-working leader said, "the extended families are often superficial, with no deep ministry; it's fun and games—picnics. Only a handful are really viable."

But even he, especially frustrated the night we talked, said some were "really walking the second mile" with their people. He said that, with or without the extended families, "there's great ministry going on all the time that we don't even hear about, people taking care of other people, giving money, praying, and all that." And, as he talked out his frustrations, it was clear that he believed they were on the right track with the concept.

A closely involved woman parishioner had a different concern. "There are a lot of people who are continually being fed, but who aren't giving out," she said. But she, too, felt the extended family program was the probable remedy for that.

One housewife, who was slightly critical of what she perceived to be "the superficiality" of some of the extended family activities, nonetheless said she wanted to join one, having held back in the beginning.

A Fuller Life Emerges

It was obvious in the ensuing months that this bold step toward meaningful church fellowship—which many in other parts of the country would describe as a form of Christian community—required more time to show its merits. Experience was required, adjustments had to be made, more individual maturity was needed. It was too soon to say this was the greatest thing to come forth in Christian living in our time, but it was also too soon to say the concept was ahead of its time. Others in different parts of the world were experimenting with similar ideas, and with some success.

However, it seemed to me as I watched that the fog and the mist were clearing; a fuller life in Christ was emerging.

There was the case of Mrs. X, a divorcee with a teenage daughter, and a member of one of the outlying extended families. She worked hard to make ends meet and to provide a good home. One of the good things about her job was that the company had provided her with a car, but it was for her only. One day she made a mistake. She let the teenage daughter use the car, and there was an accident. The company car was wrecked. It seemed certain that she would lose her job and the life she was trying to build would fall apart.

Mrs. X shared the problem with her extended family immediately. She had done wrong. She had violated company regulations. It was more her fault than her daughter's. She confessed it, and with the family members, asked God for forgiveness.

But what then? She was terrified about telling her boss. She had never been in a jam like that before. So the husband in the family's lead couple went with her to see her boss, and together they explained everything. It went far smoother than expected; and Mrs. X held together. She had someone to lean on.

But she lost the job. The company stuck to its policy.

And Mrs. X still held together. The family rallied to her with support. She learned a difficult lesson, as did her daughter, and before long she had another job. And, most importantly, she had not had to go through those days alone.

And there was the widow in another family. In the course of simple, daily living she came up against an ordinary problem that, for her, became extraordinary. She had enough resources to get by, but the exterior of her house was deteriorating. It needed painting badly, and there was no way she could afford it.

She eventually shared the problem with her extended family, they prayed about it, and before long the men in the group gathered at her home and painted the house. A simple problem was overcome by a "family."

And there were dramatic cases, too, but still in the realm of day-to-day, sometimes difficult living, and often stretching over considerable time.

Mrs. Y, who had eventually divorced her husband because of his alcoholism, regularly attended the meetings of her extended family. One night she broke the news to the other members: She had been diagnosed as having incurable cancer. They were stunned. First the divorce, then this. They knew little to do but pray with Mrs. Y—and love her.

Sometime later, through Alcoholics Anonymous, Mr. Y apparently became free of liquor. And, surprisingly, he showed up at an extended family meeting with Mrs. Y. He continued to come, and it wasn't long before he fully embraced God and committed his life to Christ. He was restored to life.

Meanwhile, Mrs. Y's health continued to deteriorate, but her spirit was soaring. She and Mr. Y were remarried just before she died. They had both been restored.

But it didn't stop there. All the members of that "family" had been touched. They had lived through a miracle. "I can't tell you how blessed my wife and I feel to have shared this experience," said the husband in the head couple.

And so it went, time after time. Low-keyed, intimate ministry was occurring. Lives that might not otherwise have touched were being shared. Emotions and bodies were healed, true families were made whole, happiness penetrated dark places.

Somehow, the common, simple, undramatic experiences seemed to overshadow the more spectacular miracles, of which there were several. For example, there was this note written to one head couple by a relatively new member:

> What a beautiful evening and what great love and prayer and fellowship we had in your home last Saturday night. I can't put into words the joy and the appreciation I felt and feel in being a part of your extended family. In spite of the heat and the rain (both of which made your hostessing more work), I thought it all was just perfect.
>
> I'm sure our extended family is precious to each one, but it means even more to one who lives alone, I'm sure.
>
> Thank you with all my heart.

It should be noted that other ministries did not stop to wait for the extended family program to get on full track. The spill-over from the concern for true fellowship had set other streams flowing, and they more or less wound their ways together, touching at many points.

There was the intercessory prayer movement, consisting of forty or more men and women who, through telephone or personal prayer chains, made daily intercessions for parishioners' needs.

There was the visitation group, a small body of people who regularly visited members of the parish who were ill or otherwise unable to go out.

There was the cooking ministry, which provided hot food for parishioners who were unable to care for themselves.

There was the transportation service, which provided travel for persons without cars who faced emergency needs.

There was the special guidance ministry, where professional assistance in financial or legal matters was given to people who could not afford it.

There was the savings association, functioning through a bank account built on unsolicited contributions from parishioners, to make interest-free loans to people facing an emergency.

There were seminarian scholarships, operating with a fund established in 1975 from contributions, to give financial support to parishioners being called to the ordained priesthood.

"So you see," Fullam said softly to the congregation one night, following a lengthy discussion of where the church seemed to be heading, "what I'm saying is that fellowship—meaning holding things in common with one another, a common life shared with Jesus Christ and with each other—is what it's all about. What you're doing in the extended families, for example, is not a fringe enterprise; it's really the whole thing. And if it doesn't lead into a loving, accepting, redemptive community where people who are not perfect, of course, can nevertheless grow to perfection with one another, bearing each other's burdens, helping each other—if we can't have that, well then, we just haven't even started. . . ."

PART THREE:

THE WORK

CHAPTER TWELVE

A Burning Coal

I stood before the large St. Paul's congregation. It was the spring of 1975.

"Why don't you come and preach next Sunday?" Fullam had asked a few days earlier just minutes before we headed our separate ways at Chicago's O'Hare Airport. It was a good opportunity to get away from the Washington newspaper grind.

"Sure, that would be fun," I had replied, perhaps a bit too hastily I thought later as I considered possible preaching subjects. I had spoken to the Darien people twice, both times at Communion breakfasts, both times with prophetic undertones. I had a nervous feeling as the hours wore on toward the weekend that my subject might be pointed, maybe uncomfortably so.

But the faces were friendly as I stood there and the congregation settled in after the sermon hymn. I had been wired with a lapel microphone that was to provide amplification and also, following St. Paul's practice, record what I had to say. It was much later when Terry told me that, inexplicably, the recording system had failed that morning for the first time. My message, delivered without notes, was not destined for other ears.

I relied primarily on two texts, both well worn, and both directly applicable to Terry Fullam and the flock committed to his charge. I backed into the first, showing how it applied to me in an upcoming venture into Christian journalism, but then turning it toward those listening to me, particularly toward their rector. I nailed it down with the second.

Most of us don't live through many moments when we have the awesome knowledge that we are saying something vitally directive, something solemnly significant, to a large group of people. Oh, we prophesy and enlighten, and it's terribly important. But then there are those rare, fragile moments when we experience something that's beyond us, when we know our words are sharply true and inspired in a special way. And even when we are aware of such a moment, the full truth of it often eludes us for a time.

First, I merely read from the first eight verses of Isaiah six:

In the year that King Uzziah died I saw the Lord sitting upon a throne, high and lifted up, and his train filled the temple. Above him stood the seraphim; each had six wings: with two he covered his face, and with two he covered his feet, and with two he flew. And one called to another and said

"Holy, holy, holy is the Lord of
hosts;
the whole earth is full of his
glory."

And the foundations of the thresholds shook at the voice of him who called, and the house was filled with smoke. And I said: "Woe is me! For I am lost; for I am a man of unclean lips, and I dwell in the midst of a people of unclean lips; for my eyes have seen the

King, the Lord of hosts!"

Then flew one of the seraphim to me, having in his hand a burning coal which he had taken with tongs from the altar. And he touched my mouth, and said: "Behold, this has touched your lips; your guilt is taken away, and your sin forgiven." And I heard the voice of the Lord saying, "Whom shall I send, and who will go for us?" Then I said, "Here am I! Send me."

Many in the congregation had heard Terry say, with variations: "The church is sent to the world; don't forget that. God *loves* the world." So more than a few of them quickly perceived my general direction. They knew that "God *so loved the world* that He gave His only Son" and that they, indeed, had been touched with "a burning coal" making them fit to "go into all the world" in His behalf. They knew, too, as I shared with them from my own recent experiences, that the most alluring temptation was to doubt the efficacy of that burning coal—the finished work of Christ on the cross and the ongoing work of the Holy Spirit in our hearts and minds.

I made several obvious points. They had been given much—a lot had been entrusted to them—and their responsibility was great. They had to determine what they were going to do with it.

Then I inched toward my goal. They had been given an extraordinary gift by Christ—a teacher—one they were probably not going to be able to keep for themselves. He was Christ's gift to the church, the wider church. They had been generous in sharing him, but they hadn't seen anything yet. The things God had given to him must be communicated far and wide.

It's interesting that I thought I was talking primarily about the Darien church's making it possible for Fullam to write books for distribution around the world. "The things you are being shown must be set down for people to read and scour, to underline, and meditate upon, to master," I said. "Neither he nor you can say, 'But we can't do that' or 'we don't know how to do that.' You *have* to find a way."

Giving Terry a shot of his own medicine, I took them immediately into Jeremiah 1:4-9, an old standby in their early development:

> Now the word of the Lord came to me saying,
> "Before I formed you in the womb I knew you,
> and before you were born I consecrated you;
> I appointed you a prophet to the nations."
> Then I said, "Ah, Lord God! Behold, I do not know how to speak, for I am only a youth." But the Lord said to me,
> "Do not say, 'I am only a youth';
> for to all to whom I send you you shall go,
> and whatever I command you you shall speak.
> Be not afraid of them,
> for I am with you to deliver you, says the Lord."
> Then the Lord put forth his hand and touched my mouth; and the Lord said to me,
> "Behold, I have put my words in your mouth. . . ."

Terry, who had moved down to one of the front seats when I began, was bent far forward, almost as though he were praying; his head nearly touched his knees. Then he straightened and looked toward the altar. I had never seen a more serious look on his face; there was not the faintest hint of a smile. Yet, strangely, I was impressed to the point of momentary distraction with the boyishness, the unusual sort of clear-facedness of his countenance for that flash of a second. The words of the Scripture had registered an astonishing impact on the big, white-robed man.

I moved my eyes from him and across the hundreds of others. I was thoroughly surprised. Tears were making little streaks and smudges on cheek after cheek. Other people had their eyes closed and their lips moved silently. Still others seemed totally impassive; they had experienced little impact apparently. It was strange.

I pressed my point to a summation. They had a mission; they knew it. And that mission would require sacrifice in the midst of great blessing. Part of that sacrifice would be in sharing their great gifts, most particularly their teacher and rector. And this definitely included the publishing of books.

As I returned to my seat, Terry led the congregation in a powerful prayer of dedication and commitment. The sanctuary seemed flooded with holiness as the service broke into worship and adoration in prayer and song.

A Steady Increase

Outreach was not new for St. Paul's, even before Fullam. "To know Christ and to make Him known" was not a hollow slogan. The nucleus that had gathered around Father Lane, while green and tentative, knew that their Lord had told them to "go . . . and make disciples of all nations," but they for the most part had not examined the phrases that followed at the end of Matthew, particularly the one that says: ". . . *teaching them* to observe all that I have commanded you. . . ."

So they had not fully anticipated what began to unfold around them in the mid-seventies. They had heard and read that "the Holy Spirit is a missionary Spirit," but they had not had the foggiest idea of the breadth of that truth. As I noted before, they liked the Fullam line that the church exists, in a sense, for those who are not yet in it;

but truthfully that thought, making them smile and nod knowingly, had not penetrated far below the surface of their consciousness.

Before accepting the Darien job, Terry traveled two or three times a month to minister in a range of settings, and the St. Paul's leaders had said they wanted him to continue that sort of thing.

In his first two years, however, he was actually away from Darien very little on speaking missions, although the fulfillment of his obligations at Barrington College did call him away regularly for several months. But gradually the missions increased. By 1975, he was away at least two days a week, and there was grumbling. "He's away too much, and we need him here," was the typical complaint. They had not seen anything yet.

In early 1975, a rather modest-looking invitation came from a Christian women's group in Washington, D.C., and Fullam sensed he should accept. The women had been meeting for a couple of years, experiencing a significant degree of renewal and reaching out to a segment of the Washington establishment that would not ordinarily be exposed to the gospel.

Somehow the group learned that my wife knew Fullam, and she was asked to introduce him at a lecture and luncheon to be held in the old and quite elegant Chevy Chase Country Club just off Connecticut Avenue.

It was a bright winter day and seventy-five women turned out to hear this eloquent Yankee in the black suit and priest's collar, the one from "that church in Connecticut where wonderful things are happening." It was a good meeting. The women were excited by Terry's lucidity and great good humor; he was their kind of preacher.

There were few, if any, who expected it, but that small meeting on the second floor of the stately club mansion set the stage for a remarkable Christian happening in the nation's capital. And it was more than a happening really; it is still going on.

Moving quickly and in great faith, the women arranged for Fullam to do a six-week New Life series designed to penetrate high-powered circles that touched the halls of government. But the short series never stopped. Fullam arranged his schedule to minister there on Mondays, speaking for two hours in the morning, meeting for lunch, and following up with questions and discussion afterward. He arrived home about five P.M. And that schedule has been in effect ever since. After the Chevy Chase Club, the meetings were moved to the mammoth National Presbyterian Church and then in the fall of 1977 to St. Luke's Methodist Church.

Attendance increased quickly in the beginning and leveled off at about four hundred men and women. The Christian minister should not be a name-dropper, and Fullam isn't, but an idea of the cross section of Washington life being reached is given by the large number of wives of congressmen and high government workers who attend regularly. It seems certain that a substantial part of the widespread Christian awareness now found in the capital has at least been influenced by Fullam's teaching.

Terry was often picked up at the airport by Mrs. Hyman L. Rickover, wife of the famous admiral and an extraordinarily committed woman. When she didn't make it, someone else equally well placed met his plane. Enthusiastic supporters of the work included Mrs. William Middendorf, wife of a former Secretary of the Navy, and Mrs. Thomas Kleppe, wife of a former Secretary of the Interior.

As far as was known, the wives of the president and the vice president had not attended the meetings, but contact was made in 1977 when Terry, his wife, and his mother attended a White House luncheon for congressmen's wives.

It was clear immediately after my talk at St. Paul's in the spring of 1975 that the parish must come to grips with Fullam's travels. Washington was just one example. The murmuring was increasing; some people felt they didn't have a full-time priest despite the fact that the staff of clergy and gifted laymen was growing. A few wanted the top man or none at all.

The vestry, at its next meeting, confronted the issue. Should they restrict their rector?

Once again, the Lord blessed them with unity, and it was agreed that Terry, and in fact St. Paul's in general, had been called to a wider ministry; a restriction would interfere with the work of the Spirit. What they had must be shared.

Fullam was authorized to spend as much time away from Darien as was required; 70 percent seemed to be the norm. He would make every effort, short of disobedience to the Lord, to be present for most Sunday services, the Wednesday night Bible studies, and the Tuesday morning Communion services.

He would before long come to the conclusion that the Lord was telling him to limit severely his participation in one-shot, ad hoc meetings and to concentrate on multi-session, multi-church meetings, especially those reaching clergy, such as diocesan conferences. This was solely for the sake of efficiency and proper stewardship of time and resources.

The presiding bishop of the Episcopal church, John M. Allin, once said he believed Fullam carried out more missions in a year than anyone in the Episcopal church.

He should know, but the truth of the statement is difficult to prove. In 1976, however, Terry ministered in Washington, Oregon, California, Arizona, Texas, Louisiana, Florida, every state in the East, and into Canada. Many of those missions were to large groups of clergy and diocesan conferences. They included every Episcopal church in the United States with any sort of national or regional influence in renewal.

His ministry abroad grew quickly, taking in several nations of Africa, Israel, Jordan, Syria, Turkey, Greece, Britain, and several provinces of Canada.

Yes, the apostle was sent out.

The Issue of Authority

The pain was felt fairly quickly. All in St. Paul's recognized Fullam's special gifts and his call; but not all could handle it. And they didn't lack justification, at least in part. When Terry was away, he couldn't be in Darien ministering to their needs.

In fact, after years of close observation and months of fine-detailed searching, this was actually the only problem of any substance I found in God's miracle in Darien. It was seemingly the one weakness, and the question inevitably grew: Was it an Achilles' heel?

I probed the issue with several of the leaders and others who held no leadership position. Pessimism was not supreme, but they were unanimous on the importance of the question.

"The one problem at St. Paul's," one leader said, "is Terry and his mission to the world. Everything here centers around him. You might almost say he's the king—which really isn't true, of course, but you see the point. We're seriously hobbled by his absence. When he's gone there's no authority. He takes it with him."

The issue could not have been defined more bluntly

than that. Others said it less forcefully, but that was their point. A number of them believed, to one degree or another, that the absence of their very strong leader impeded the rest of the ministry. Some went so far as to say there was a feeling during Terry's absence that no one was in charge.

"We need a shepherd on site with real authority when Terry's away," said a woman. "Some people have gotten hurt."

Her point was explained in bits and pieces from several others, including some working frequently "on site." It seemed that those who actually had been given authority to act were reluctant to use it when the rector was away; it was as though their reinforcement had been taken away. Then, with something of a vacuum having been created, a man said, "Ego-driven people start vying with one another, making end runs around each other, and they just take over. It's destructive."

Many of the parishioners felt this was a gross exaggeration. "Sure, we all miss Terry when he's away; he's a terribly powerful man. But things don't come to a stop. There are others who work, and work hard, and the ministry gets done."

I believe this would be a majority view if every parishioner could be questioned. Satisfaction would not be total on this issue, but outright discontent would receive little voice.

There was another dimension to the problem, however, and it too merited exploration. There were a handful at the leadership level who felt Fullam too frequently returned from a mission and countermanded actions taken by responsible people during his absence. "There is no authority without Terry," one said. "He needs to give his authority to someone else. There are slippages in management."

I felt the last sentence was meaningful. Quite understandably many people, who have little history in any body-of-Christ life simply because there have been so few cases of it in recent generations, couldn't avoid falling back into a business syndrome when dealing with difficulties. They unwittingly equated church management with business management.

Nevertheless, the criticism and the overall matter of authority deserved discussion.

The afternoon sun was very low on the horizon and casting slanting lines across his living room as Fullam and I talked. We were only skirting the fringes of the subject when, without priming, came a most important remark to enlighten Christian understanding.

"There's one thing we have learned out of all this," he said. "There's no transferring the anointing."

He smiled, put his hand to his forehead, and then chuckled softly. "Even though I'm not here much of the time, there's absolutely no question in anybody's mind who's rector of this place—you know? It's kind of an authority which I think the Lord has given me. And I don't have any problem with it—I rest at ease with it. But I can't transfer it—I mean—it doesn't depend on me. It's not anything I can give to anybody else."

There was the answer. *"It doesn't depend on me."* The anointing—the authority—had been given by God to him. Only God could transfer it. And only the one to whom it was being transferred could take it. Terry Fullam couldn't do it for God, and Terry Fullam couldn't receive it for someone else.

Then I saw that deep quality again—the deepest one perhaps that I'd seen in Fullam. He was willing to wait for God to work this out. He knew the principles of plural leadership they were operating on were correct. And he knew that if they were obedient, if they tried—and waited—God would work those principles out in them. It was that very elusive quality of trust—and patience.

I knew, watching him in the fading afternoon light, that he was not going to become rattled by some rough spots in the road if he knew they were on the right road. The Lord would not let the good work He had begun in them fall apart merely because of some confusion about authority, its delegation, and the use of it. The right people, for that moment at least, were in place and Christ the head would bring them into maturity as they did the jobs set before them, receiving His gifts "to equip the saints for the work of ministry . . . until we all . . . attain to mature manhood."

Fullam's extreme patience was also seen in one of the ministries to which he was "sent out"—leadership in the Episcopal Charismatic Fellowship, aimed at assisting charismatic renewal within the church. Outwardly, the first several years of that work seemed to border on failure more than anything else. Struggles with direction, structure, and personnel ended year after year in frustration.

But, despite the appearance, there was movement—Episcopalians in many places were helped toward renewal—and God was at work in the leadership of the E.C.F. For several years Fullam was prominent as a member of the board of directors, where I served with him, and as a featured teacher at most of the regional and national conferences.

In 1977, his visibility and responsibility were heightened when, following a painfully fought-out reorganization, he accepted direct oversight as president.

As he counseled absolute submission to the leading of the Holy Spirit and patience, the E.C.F. was emitting signs of increased service to the wider church.

As for Fullam the teacher, the tempo picked up. There were historic conferences in South Africa, in Kansas City, and in Canterbury, England; there were nitty-gritty seminars and workshops in the heart of Kansas and the plains of Texas; there were grinding, daily meetings in the little-known communities of New Zealand; there were the intense taping sessions for a weekly television series by the Christian Broadcasting Network; there were frank and delicate sessions with the hierarchy of the Episcopal church. Doors opened everywhere. But hadn't Jeremiah hinted as much?

"Do not say, 'I am only a youth';
for to all to whom I send you you
   shall go,
And whatever I command you you shall
   speak. . . ."

CHAPTER THIRTEEN

Ministry to the World

The beginning was so simple as to escape memory.

Jan Leaton merely thought it would be nice to record some of the excellent teaching they were receiving. So she took a small cassette machine to church.

One never became quite accustomed to it. A snap would pierce the hush, and people would jump. It was Jan and her recorder. You could almost hear her fingers scurrying to flip the cassette; then came a softer snap; it was running again. She captured as much as she could.

At home she made duplicate tapes, a laborious, time-consuming process. And they were swept up faster than she could turn them out. But at least the ministry was being spread around.

It became clear that Jan's initiative had been prophetic. The tapes were changing lives, according to reports filtering back to the church, but more efficiency was needed. So Mark Hessian, an electrician, installed professional recording equipment in the church at cost, and the tape ministry entered phase two. But he soon found he was giving twenty to thirty hours a week to the operation, and even that wasn't enough. Parishioners were devouring the recorded teachings but, perhaps more importantly, they were starting to reach distant places—church groups beginning to dabble in renewal, home meetings, and individuals suffering from a lack of ministry.

Phase three came when the church recognized it needed two full-time people, along with a steadily increasing crew of volunteers, to meet the demands of sales and a church tape library.

A recent tabulation showed one thousand two hundred tapes a month were being sold, on a nonprofit basis, with many hundreds more being lent through the library. Sixty percent were being sent beyond the Darien area, even overseas.

The full impact of such an outreach is difficult to measure. But there are little, heart-warming stories, and there are dramatic accounts traceable to it.

A tiny group of eager Christians, for example, gathered every Thursday morning in a large, but underutilized Episcopal church in Morristown, New Jersey, to listen to tapes from St. Paul's. Their sessions were intense and serious, notes were taken studiously, and the teachings were debated enthusiastically. The spiritual growth of the individuals—as few as they were—defied secular explanation. And one could almost see their hearts burning within them as they clung to this flame of hope.

The other extreme in drama occurred in faraway Rhodesia, a center of strife whose only hope may be the gospel. Only the skimpiest details could be obtained, and they from an Anglican bishop from neighboring South Africa.

As reconstructed, the drama began with the faithful determination of an unknown woman who attended Fullam's teachings in Washington. After hearing him, she purposed to buy four cassette tapes of his ministry each week, to be sent to various places, presumably abroad and

possibly all to Rhodesia. At any rate, according to Bishop
Nutall, the tapes were eventually "all over the country,"
or so it seemed.

One or more reportedly fell into the hands of a son of the
Rhodesian prime minister, Ian Smith, and he was
converted, whether solely through the tapes or not was
unknown. He, in turn, made the tapes available to his
father and, as told by Bishop Nutall, the prime minister
was converted to Christ.

"I had no idea our tapes were being sent to Rhodesia,"
Fullam said, "until the bishop told me that story in
England."

And, of course, he had no idea what the reported events
would mean in the seemingly insoluble distress of
Rhodesia, but the witness by tape, begun so humbly
several years earlier on a hand-held recorder, was
apparently reaching to the ends of the earth.

Parish Renewal Weekends

"Small beginnings" seemed to be a household phrase in
Darien. Almost without exception, the church eased or
backed into its most significant ministries—an indication
that it was quite likely following, not pushing.

The parish renewal weekends, probably its most telling
outreach over the long run, came pretty much that way.
People in other parishes began to hear of the "unusual
things" going on in that "little church in Darien," and they
came to investigate. Before long they were coming with
delegations from their own parishes. And then, in time,
they were more or less getting under foot. Inefficiency,
and possibly even disorder, threatened.

It was time to set up a schedule where the visitors'
needs could be properly met, and the possibilities for
renewal more clearly set forth. It was time for organized
parish renewal weekends. Delegations could register in

advance, arrive late Friday for a time together that evening, meet all day Saturday, share with families and groups more intimately that night, and worship with the entire church at the Sunday morning service. All aspects of church life—from vestry operations to extended families—could be covered methodically, and the guests could learn through participation how a caring fellowship lived.

The special weekends could be conducted twice a year, each accommodating three hundred visitors from all over the country—although twice that number sought to come and there were hopes of increasing the capacity. They could return to their parishes to share what they'd experienced—adopting, modifying, or discarding, according to what the Lord was doing in their local situations.

Success was instantaneous. People came literally from the farthest parts of the country—and from abroad—to see if there was something they could take back to their home churches to enhance renewal.

Jonathan Simonds, a parishioner from St. Peter's Church in Morristown, New Jersey, returned from such a weekend and his face was flushed with excitement. "It's beautiful!" he said. "I've never seen anything like it."

Helen Bailey, a member of the same delegation, spoke enthusiastically of the worship experience. "The Spirit just lifted us," she said, raising her hands, palms upward, "and we really found what it was like to worship in a body."

Responses like this gladdened the people at St. Paul's, but later began to stir concern. They sensed something was not quite right.

Two of the concerned were Fullam and Gordon Lyle, who had begun to travel some with Terry on missions, and they saw with a different perspective from out in the countryside.

"I think it was Gordon who picked up on this first," Terry said much later. "He saw that in many cases we were merely increasing the frustration level of a lot of people. They were coming here and getting excited and then going back to lifelessness."

And once again they were face to face with a peculiarity of many denominational churches, and particularly the Episcopal church. Renewal in a parish seemed virtually impossible unless the rector was renewed first. Fullam had many times said, "A rector can't necessarily bring renewal, but he can sure block it."

It was a matter of structure. Very little was going to reach the congregation as a whole without the rector's participation. Individuals might be renewed, and even little groups might form, but full life in the Spirit parishwide was difficult if the rector wasn't moving with it.

"Gordon had been a key figure in the parish renewal seminars," Fullam said, "and it was he who had the definite insight that we should work with the clergy. So once again, he was a 'midwife,' a role he played with several ministries around here. He had the vision for conducting seminars for clergymen and their wives before trying to help their parishes. He wrote the brochure, did a lot of the groundwork—of course, he had a lot of people working with him—and he and his wife, Connie, became sort of the presiding elders for these new seminars."

One of the first concerns was scheduling them at a time when up to thirty priests from parishes showing interest could get away for a few intense days. So, exploiting Fullam's availability early in the week, they arranged to begin the sessions on Monday evening with a dinner and a talk by Terry, placing the visitors in parish homes for the night. Tuesday opened with participation in the regular

Tuesday morning Communion service to guarantee a worship experience with a full congregation, followed by sessions on various aspects of renewal throughout the day and evening, including talks by lay leaders. The meetings continued through Wednesday, culminating in the regular Wednesday night Bible study, and concluded with celebration of the Eucharist Thursday morning, breakfast, and a time of sharing together.

The impact of the seminars was perhaps best indicated by a priest from New Brunswick, Canada, who confided emotionally after the Tuesday morning Eucharist service, "I feel I've been to church for the first time in my life. I've come into contact with God."

The results were so dramatic and the prospects for renewal so improved that the St. Paul's leaders decided the parish renewal weekends would thenceforth be confined essentially to delegations from churches whose rectors had attended one of the four yearly seminars and who accompanied the lay delegation.

"The frustration level among the lay people has been reduced considerably," said Fullam, "and we believe we're on the right track."

Evangelism in the Church

For several years, I'd had a nagging notion perched on my shoulder just back of the peripheral vision line. It came almost into sight a time or two, but quickly retreated. I knew it had to do with evangelism—not standard-brand, baby-doctor evangelism, not street preaching, not house calling. It had to do with the full church, but not the traditional Sunday-night evangelistic meetings and not big rallies. Those were good tools, and they had been well used at times in church history, but there was that notion. . . .

The Lord intended for His church, not isolated

individuals, to be His main instrument of evangelism. That's sort of what it was saying.

And then one day it happened. All the lights went on, and I got a good look at my nagging notion. Sitting encompassed by the body at an ordinary service at St. Paul's Church—with no special evangelistic preaching, no altar calls—the reality of the missionary Spirit swept across me like a breath. The understanding went something like this:

The Holy Spirit converts . . . the Holy Spirit also gives life to the church. . . . When the Holy Spirit is given full reign in a church, He manifests himself in a variety of ways, all pointing toward the Savior. . . . Indeed, the Holy Spirit is the *Life* of the church, in the sense that He is the working arm of the Trinity on earth. . . . If a church is full of that Life, He will give himself to all if they open themselves in the least. . . . The very Life of the church will convert people, causing them to embrace Jesus Christ as they sit in their pews, even when no one is working overtly toward that end.

It's not quite as simple as that, of course. There must be the preaching of the Word at some point. People are saved through faith, and faith comes through the preaching of Christ.[1] The Spirit uses the preaching, with the sealing, the clinching—the rebirth—coming as He blows where He wills, "and you hear the sound of it, but you do not know whence it comes or whither it goes; so it is with every one who is born of the Spirit."[2]

There is probably an element of this in the apostle Paul's First Letter to the Corinthians, chapter fourteen, verse twenty-four. He is emphasizing the importance of prophecy in the church and says, "If all prophesy, and an unbeliever or outsider enters, he is convicted by all, he is called to account by all, the secrets of his heart are disclosed; and so, falling on his face, he will worship God

[1]Romans 10:17.   [2]John 3:8.

and declare that God is really among you."

And that's what happened. The most powerful evangelism imaginable occurred at St. Paul's when nothing particularly "evangelistic" was taking place outwardly. Furthermore, people were baptized in the Holy Spirit as they sat in the congregation when such an occurrence was not even being discussed. And people were healed, especially inwardly and in their relationships. They were touched by the Spirit even as He gave life to the church.

This, I realized, was what the Lord had meant when He told Terry at the age of eighteen that he was to "nourish and beget the life of God in the souls of men."

And it was reassuring to find this experience borne out by the Nicene Creed, which churches throughout the world repeat week after week but so rarely embrace in its fullness: "We believe in the Holy Spirit, *the Lord, the giver of life.* . . ." The church fathers had fully appreciated Christ's thorough identification with the Spirit at work within the "one holy catholic and apostolic church."

It was through these experiences that I came to see one of the Darien church's most important and most unplanned ministries of outreach—its worship services. This included the regular Sunday services, but probably the most significant on this level was the Sunday night service that eventually unfolded.

It began small, as usual, in the St. Paul's sanctuary, but attendance soon made that site impossible, and the congregation was invited to a little-used church in nearby Stamford, Emmanuel Episcopal Church. It seemed ideal, and before long four hundred people and more were attending regularly, a large number of them from churches other than St. Paul's. While the congregation included people of all kinds and ages, young people seemed especially attracted, and the service took on a special enthusiasm and spontaneity.

Many, particularly young adults, said that, for a range of reasons, they had been reluctant to go to regular Sunday morning church services, whether at St. Paul's or elsewhere. "Church" put them off. But they heard about the informality and gusto of the Emmanuel meetings and gave them a try. With many of them, the pattern was to test the Sunday night service, have an encounter with the Lord, see that only good things resulted, and then branch out to include a regular Sunday meeting, either at St. Paul's or another Christ-centered church.

So, the Sunday night service, while definitely a gathering of believers, most of them ardent, was also a form of outreach. New people were ministered to every week.

Fullam presided regularly at the night services as well as at the morning when he was not out of town, usually assisted by one or more of the three other St. Paul's priests—Joe Gatto, Bob Weeks, and Martyn Minns. In addition, visiting ministers were periodically scheduled to preach, adding an extra dimension of background and style.

Meanwhile, the regular Sunday morning services and those at midweek continued to reach new people from near and far, most particularly those with some church background who were searching for a closer walk with the Lord.

The fellowship of believers continued to suggest itself as the Lord's more perfect instrument of evangelism, demonstrating anew the truth of the apostle Paul's words:

> Yes, to this day whenever Moses is read a veil lies
> over their minds; but when a man turns to the Lord
> the veil is removed. Now the Lord is the Spirit, and

where the Spirit of the Lord is, there is freedom. And we all, with unveiled face, beholding the glory of the Lord, are being changed into his likeness from one degree of glory to another; for this comes from the Lord who is the Spirit.[3]

Heart-warming Outreach

Jeanne Tinsley is an exuberant woman, even jolly, but she can cry as quickly as she can laugh and will sometimes seem to do both simultaneously. Compassionate people often are that way.

As the Lord moved thoroughly upon St. Paul's Church, she, like so many, soaked up the blessings, attending meeting upon meeting and returning home, apparently waiting for something, but she wasn't sure what. Then began another of those slow slides into a ministry, an outreach that any speculating man would be sure brings a smile of gratitude to the face of Jesus.

"About a half-dozen of us concluded at the same time that, while it was fun to be fed and fed and fed at St. Paul's," she said, "we had become spiritually obese. We needed to get out and work it off."

The answer for them, they sensed, was to start spreading the blessings around by visiting people who could never get to the church. "We wanted to let the light of Jesus shine through us," Jeanne said, beaming.

So a group, numbering up to six, began visiting a section at a huge mental institution each week, ministering in song and simple conversation—sharing the good news and its effects on their lives—to twenty-five patients. Since they could reach only one of many sections at the institution, other churches later made commitments to minister in other buildings. And as more ministerial feet got wet, similar groups followed with visits to a nearby private mental hospital, to a public

---

[3]2 Cor. 3:15-18.

hospital, to a nursing home, and even to a prison.

Mrs. Tinsley, who once was a professional musical entertainer, meanwhile joined a friend to begin visits to homes for the aged, ministering primarily through song and sharing to a different home each week. This heartbreaking work eventually became a grind, she confessed, and the day came when she wanted to stay at home and rest. But a tiny spark of duty pierced her conscience and she gathered up her little hymnals to head out.

"When I opened the door of that home," she said later, "and saw how happy those people were that we had come—many in wheelchairs, people who rarely have any visitors—it was as though a mantle of love had fallen. I felt engulfed with love for those precious people. I have never felt so strongly that His love was flowing through me."

It was then that the bright laughter and tears flowed together. "We learned again that, by serving others, it is we who are blessed."

The same sort of results came from the faithful visits of Phil March, David Rust, and others to the Federal prison at nearby Danbury. Working through the Yokefellow program, they went to the institution one night every two weeks to share the gospel and enter into fellowship with inmates. Deep commitments and strong relationships developed, involving such diverse people as a former national union leader, a former Mafia figure, a man once intimately involved with wheeler-dealer Bobby Baker, and men convicted of well-publicized white-collar crimes.

This ministry even led to a modified Faith Alive weekend at the prison, in which a team of men and women were received behind steel doors for a lively day and a half of witnessing, song, and prayer.

Faith Alive provided an effective outlet for other

people at St. Paul's committed to the notion that every Christian is a minister. This is a national movement under which teams of lay teachers, preachers, and just ordinary people travel to other communities to meet, eat, and witness with members of other parishes, the purpose being to share the reality of a faith that is "alive." The list of participants from Darien in this brand of personal low-key outreach is long.

And that's the way it went.

—A psychiatrist-psychologist team placed itself under the church, counseling and teaching others how to counsel in certain cases, eventually establishing a Christian clinic in Darien.

—The vestry engaged in periodic retreats with vestries from other parishes, providing opportunities for free exchanges on purposes and methods.

—Many parishioners became active in the Marriage Encounter movement that has been extraordinarily effective across the nation refounding and reaffirming marriages, those seriously (and not so seriously) in trouble.

—A Mobile Ministry of high-school and college-age people was established to minister around New England through music and witness.

—The church gave strong financial and logistical support, including office space and salary for a full-time worker, to the Young Life ministry to high-school students in the area.

—A bookstore was established to provide reliable Christian literature to people from a wide area.

—Twenty-two women with appropriate temperaments and knowledge banded together to relieve the impossible burden of incoming telephone traffic to the church from people all over the country with an assortment of needs defying imagination.

—The congregation entered into the custom of setting aside a Sunday at the end of each summer on which to commission and send out as ministers of the gospel those young people bound for college away from home.

Carl Rodemann had that crinkly-eyed look again as he shared with a group of visitors a concept that St. Paul's Church committed itself to—"being a launching pad for ministries." He spoke of moving from theory into practice.

"How do we get our pet dinosaur to move—aside from just noisily kicking it?" he asked. "There are no simple answers to this, and there is no cookbook to give all the recipes that apply to each church."

He went on to make clear his view that his church, St. Paul's, to which so many were turning as a model, "still has some unfinished business to do."

"Terry has often reminded us," he said, "that the command to go into all the world is a universal command—unless you have personally had a revelation that says you are exempt. That does not necessarily mean you have to go to Africa. For some this means visiting a lonely, old person in the next apartment or around the corner from the church, or recognizing what your ministry is at the place where you work."

He paused for a fraction of a second and his face turned extraordinarily serious. "I think what all of this does mean—the going out—it means a posture and an attitude of an entire parish and each member, to be poised and ready and willing to go out wherever called or needed. I think what it means is recognizing that personal growth results from going and giving. It means that we grow in strength with exercise—and recognize that there's a real danger of growing spiritually fat if we're only concerned with being fed.

"It means"—his voice was even and paced—"recognizing that we're called upon not to *come* to church, but to *be* the church, seven days a week, wherever we are dispersed."

There obviously were some hurdles ahead.

CHAPTER FOURTEEN

The Living Temple

Terry Fullam, it has become obvious, does not jump to conclusions. Indeed, he talks very little about conclusions. "We have no continuing city,"[1] he likes to say. "We are a pilgrim people,[2] a people on the move." Things have not been completed.

Similarly, he does not change his mind abruptly, having extraordinary faith in his manner of arriving at decisions and understandings in the first place.

So when I heard him say, "I've changed my mind," I paid close attention. We were at the Marianist Apostolic Center in Glencoe, Missouri, in the spring of 1977 when he said it—in front of about forty people attending a so-called charismatic leaders' conference. It was one of the few times I'd heard him speak a bit haltingly, as though he were still sorting out his thoughts, as though he hadn't fully solved his problem. He didn't have all the answers and, being a careful man who doesn't often sound off prematurely, that made him uncomfortable.

Over a few weeks, he continued to assemble his thoughts, and in dabs and dribbles he tried them out, again revealing the progressive development that has characterized so much of his ministry—a characteristic

---

[1]Hebrews 13:14.   [2]Hebrews 11:13.

found, in fact, in the history of God's dealing with His people. The hearing—and resultant articulation—of even the most obedient follower is not yet perfect.

But soon it was time, even though not every answer was in place, and he stood before the full congregation at St. Paul's, uttered the final phrases of his sermon prayer, and stared for several seconds at the people.

"I've changed my mind."

He paused, and the congregation waited expectantly. "Now it's not the first time that I have changed my mind, and I suspect it will not be the last time. Sometimes the change of mind comes very rapidly; something happens or you learn something that changes the whole perspective, and you have to revise your thinking about it. But sometimes your mind is changed slowly, gradually, almost imperceptibly, as this happens, or this or that is obeserved, so that little by little you find your thinking revised.

"I know that during 1976 I underwent a change in thinking."

He had traveled far and wide—rarely less than four days a week and often five or more—and had ministered at just about every level.

"What I have seen," he said again, "has led me to a revision in my thinking. I do not now believe that God is interested in renewing the Episcopal church."

The silence was leaden. And the faintest of smiles touched his lips. "Now that may come as a shock to you."

The sharp understatement relieved the tension slightly. "But everywhere around I see the unmistakable signs of death. I don't know whether you know it or not, but a former bishop of this diocese has said that within ten years, one half of the Episcopal churches in the state of Connecticut may have to be closed unless something happens. And I don't know whether you know this or not, but we have lost—that is, our particular branch of the church, the Episcopal church—we have lost one member every five minutes for ten years. There's death everywhere in the church."

He quickly added that, at the same time, there were remarkable evidences of the grace and power of God in many places and that he knew the gates of hell would not ultimately prevail against the church.[3]

"But I am also convinced," he declared, "that we are witnessing, in our own lifetime, the death of much of the institution that we have called the church."

He paused for a second, and added just a shade lower, "And I am prepared to dance at its funeral."

Recalling the Bible's warning against pouring new wine into old wine sacks that had become stiff and brittle, he cast doubt on whether the Lord was interested in revitalizing old brittle structures "that never really were responsive to His Holy Spirit anyway."

Mixing his metaphors, he went on: "It's not only in our denomination—it's true in them all—such barnacles have clung to the bark of faith that they might well have sunk the ship.

"I'm reminded," he said, taking them by memory into the Scriptures, "of the word of Jesus in Matthew fifteen when someone came to Him and said, 'Master, why do your followers ignore the tradition of the elders,' and Jesus answered by asking another question. 'Why do the elders,' He said, 'transgress the commandments of God by their traditions?' Then He quoted the Old Testament and said, 'This people honors me with their lips, but their heart is far from me.'[4]

"And then He made this astute observation: 'Every tree which my Father has not planted will be uprooted.'[5]

"There's no way to stop the death and the decay of that which in its fundamental root is not responsive to the will

---

[3]Matthew 16:18.   [4]Matthew 15:1-9.   [5]Matthew 15:13.

of God."

At that moment, there was a distinct shift in gears, a shift away from the heaviness of negativism toward the positive, which was the substance of his change of mind:

> There are so many aspects of church life that seem so alien to how the Scriptures describe the church that one might ask the question, "Is there any continuity between the church described in the pages of the New Testament and the churches that exist today, in any denomination at all?"
>
> *I'm convinced that God is not renewing the church but that He is indeed restoring the church in our day.*
>
> Now that may seem to you a distinction without substance, but I believe there's a difference between renewing old, dead structures—pouring life into structures that are not responsive—and the restoring of an authentic church; that is, the body of Christ, a church where the divisions of the world do not bring divisions within the body. The divisions between rich and poor, between black and white, between male and female—all of those distinctions which are absolute in the world can be overcome within the body of Christ. I think God is restoring the church in our day.

Fullam had said something similar to this, although not in any detail, at the parish's annual meeting and was confronted immediately by a man who asked, "Is what you've said tonight a declaration of independence from the Episcopal church?"

The question was reasonable. He could have sounded as though he were saying that the Episcopal church and all the others were dead, and that he wanted to get out before they sank and took St Paul's down with them.

"I want to put to rest, forever, that this is not my meaning," Fullam told the congregation. "I was called of God into the ministry of the Episcopal church and it is my intention, by the grace of God, to die in that ministry. It is not my plan nor my will ever to see this congregation withdraw from the Episcopal church."

He shrugged his shoulders slightly, looked at the lectern and then back to the crowd, his voice lowering a bit. "I know enough about independent Christianity to know it is not any more desirable than the fellowship of God's people called the Episcopal church. There are problems everywhere.

"You see"—his hand moved up to shoulder level in a half wave—"God isn't interested in renewing the Methodists, or the Roman Catholics, Baptists, or Episcopalians—or the independents. He's interested in restoring a church—one church. We say every Sunday, 'I believe in one holy catholic and apostolic church,'[6] but the church as you and I know it, and as it exists, does not manifest that belief. But God is doing it nonetheless. We're finding ancient distinctions overcome through the mighty power and the works of the Holy Spirit in our day."

When pressed on this later, Terry acknowledged he did not at that time have a clear picture of what the restored church would be like, particularly since he apparently was saying that denominations would remain.

"I just don't know," he said, wrinkling his brow. "There are so many things we don't know. But it is certain we don't have that 'one holy catholic and apostolic church' now, and it is certain that we have departed from the church described in the New Testament."

Fullam had long been troubled by the fact that in a city like Boston, say, there was no such thing as "the Boston church." There was the Presbyterian church, the

[6]Nicene Creed.

Episcopal church, the Roman Catholic church, the
Assemblies of God; whereas the New Testament speaks
of the "church at Antioch," the "church at Ephesus," and
so on. Somewhere in there, he suspected, was a clue for
today. Perhaps there should be "the church at Boston,"
with all the branches working together, planning
together, helping one another, but meeting in different
bodies—perhaps even along denominational lines—for
the simple fact that it would be impossible to
accommodate a regular meeting of the full church.

Maybe it was merely an attitudinal matter.

"I just don't know at this time," he said, with just a hint
of exasperation touching his long-proven patience.

"Go Through the Gates"

In the early months of 1977, Fullam spent a lot of time
seeking clearer understanding about God's purpose with
the Episcopal church, with St. Paul's particularly, and
with the wider church. He prayed; he read the Bible.

"Lord," he said in the quietness of his study at home,
"show me what you want me to see about your work in this
place. Put it together for me in a way that I've not seen
before."

And the Lord responded. He was directed to the
sixty-second chapter of the Book of Isaiah and then into
verse ten:

Go through, go through the gates,
   prepare the way for the people;
build up, build up the highway,
   clear it of stones,
   lift up an ensign over the peoples.

The context was clear; the prophecy from the sixtieth
chapter to the end was dealing with the restoration of

God's people. Israel—the people of the old covenant—was in just about the same condition that he perceived the church—the people of the new covenant—generally to be in. It had fallen away from the foundation of the covenant promises. It had fallen away from the worship of the true God. The people of God had fallen into dependence on their own wisdom, their own ideas, while the Scripture made it abundantly clear that it was not by their own might or power that God's work was to be done, but by the Holy Spirit.[7]

The prophet, pointing the way to restoration, was vigorously exhorting the people, and Fullam perceived at that moment that the exhortation drove straight at his own earlier prayer. It gave clear direction for today's church in the form of five imperatives, which he later shared with the people of St. Paul's.

"Now in Hebrew and also in Greek," he said, "when a writer wants to make a point emphatically, he repeats it. Jesus did that: *'Verily, verily,* I say unto you'—the same idea. *'Go through, go through* the gates.'

"There's absolutely no going on with God," he said firmly, "if you're a Christian or if you're a church, without the notion that you have to step out—go through the gates, move out. Now of course, there's a coming to the Lord first, and there's a moving out from Him. But, you see, we are talking about dealing with a God who is on the move. You cannot stand up, and stand still, and serve God—because our God is a God on the move. He is calling you to come to Him and to go out from Him. Go into all the world, Jesus said, and proclaim the gospel.[8] You can't do that standing still. You have to move."

He paused and the words seemed to hang over the congregation. "So the first imperative is 'go through the gates.' Now that need not be simple physical distance as one would traverse a mile or two. It can be a psychological

[7]Zechariah 4:6.   [8]Mark 16:15.

distance—the idea that we have to go out from our notions, our ideas, of what the church is, or what we think we should be doing. There isn't *always* a physical motion out through the gates."

Next in the prophet's list was "prepare the way for the people." What would that mean for St. Paul's?

"We are to prepare a way for the people," Fullam declared, citing the church's theme of knowing Christ and making Him known, "that they might come to Him, that they might know Him. It's interesting in the Acts of the Apostles that the early Christians were called people of 'the Way.' Jesus, of course, said concerning himself, 'I am the way.'[9] We are to prepare, then, ways for people to come to the Lord. We are to build bridges into other people's lives—bridges of friendship and trust—that the Lord Jesus might walk across that bridge into the life of a person who does not know Him. Constantly, this is our endeavor; it is an imperative."

He raised his Bible in front of his face again and pressed ahead. "But then it says, 'build up, build up the highway.' In the King James it says 'cast up the highway.' Raise up a way, a highway. That's what we are to build—a way for people to come to the Lord. We are to make it so clear that the wayfarer, though a stranger, will not be lost. We are to erect, if you will, a road because we are people of the Way.

"The Scripture tells us that here we have no continuing city, that we are not to expect that we are to settle down. We are sojourners. That's the biblical word for it—sojourners, people who have no settled dwelling place. We are to recognize ourselves as a pilgrim people—a people on the move, a people seeking to increase the ranks of those headed for the kingdom of the Lord. We're on the Way, and we're to build up the highway."

---

[9]John 14:6.

Turning to the fourth imperative—"clear it of stones"—he took his listeners back to the fifty-seventh chapter of Isaiah to look at a parallel passage: "Build up, build up, prepare the way, remove every *obstruction* from my people's way."

"The clearing of the highway of stones," he said, "means that we are to give effort to removing obstacles in the way of people coming into a full faith and life with the Lord Jesus Christ. Remove the obstacles, the things that are in the way of the people who are coming." They might include a number of things, big and small, hindrances that have nothing to do with God's will for a person's life—from denominational conflicts and personal biases to such simple matters as inconsiderate treatment and difficulties in parking or seating.

"And then," Fullam said, "there's a fifth imperative in this remarkable verse: go, prepare, build up, clear the stones, and *'lift up an ensign over the peoples.'* "

He lowered his Bible. "The word 'ensign' means a banner of identification. We get the word 'insignia' from the same roots. An insignia is a badge of identification."

He flipped several pages backward in his Bible. " 'Lift up an ensign over the peoples.' " He flipped several more and continued to talk. "We are told in the eleventh chapter of Isaiah what that ensign is that we are to lift up. We are to raise up the ensign of the son of Jesse."

His hand landed on the passage. "Chapter eleven, verse ten: 'In that day the root of Jesse shall stand as an ensign to the people; him shall the nations seek, and his dwellings shall be glorious.' "

He lowered the Bible and looked up. "Those of you who are familiar with biblical terminology know that 'the root of Jesse' is one of the designations of the coming Messiah, the Lord Jesus Christ, the root of Jesse, the root of David, the Coming One. We are to lift up an ensign over the people. Jesus said, 'If I be lifted up I will draw all people unto myself.'[10] It's not that we have to go out and make people come. We need to lift Him so high that people will see His light and people who have lost their way will find it again. We need to lift Him so high that His love may provide a warmth for those who are lonely and lost and feel forsaken. We do not need so much to be a trophy case for saints having reached perfection as a hospital where people come to wholeness. That's the call upon us and we are to lift up the Lord Jesus Christ in the midst of His people so that at no time will anyone have the slightest question of whose people we are, whom we serve, and where we're going."

He stopped, and his eyes moved across the congregation for several moments.

"I wonder," he said, slowing his delivery ever so slightly, "if the message is as clear to you as it is to me. God says, 'St. Paul's, I have a job for you to do. I want you to go through the gates, move out. I want you to prepare the way for the people. I want you to build up a highway. I want you to clear it of any stones and obstacles and obstructions. And I want you to raise up an ensign over the people, that they may see whose people you are, and seeing they will believe and fall on their faces and worship, giving their lives and service to the King of kings and the Lord of lords.' "

The Course Is Altered

The time was crucial at St. Paul's. The increase in communicants was astounding, quadrupling and more in four years. The number of Sunday services alone had grown to four. It was clear that the church must respond to this growth in some way. But crucial to that response was a clearer perception of what God's intent for them was. What was He going to do with them? This would

---

[10]John 12:32.

govern the matter of accommodating growth.

In secular organizations, this would have been crisis time. The church was snagging on several points of frustration in its efforts to move forward. The leaders and most of the parish knew that they had received an unusual calling, but they often found themselves knee-deep in quicksand as they tried to work out that calling. There were disappointments and setbacks, almost all involving the problems of growth and of people learning to get along with people. But they pushed ahead with their commitment to work for the restoration of the church.

The climax came in the spring of 1977—a moment of threatening darkness and the smell of defeat, followed by a burst of light and the sweet fragrance of victory. The Lord first closed many distracting doors, then set St. Paul's on an altered course with a new, yet ancient, concept of the church of Jesus Christ. Things were never to be the same.

Fullam provided an insightful analysis of the often confusing events and the emerging concept, being the one person placed so as to see the shaping and merging of the various spiritual and physical elements:

It became clear that we needed to respond to this growth in some way. Though God had shown me the general direction for this church and the end result, He had not told me just how we were to achieve it. I was not given a clearly designed program to implement step by step. The Lord did not want St. Paul's to be built around me. And lest that happen, He systematically removes me from this place 70 percent of the time.

The Lord showed us at the very beginning He wanted to lead this church in unity. The vestry would have to trust that the Lord would lead us in

discussions as a vestry, and we would have to listen
to each other—be submitted to the Lord, but also
submitted to each other so that we could hear His
voice. We had some of the original Connecticut
Yankees in this place! I wasn't sure even God could
unite them. It has been astounding to see how people
of intense personality and strong opinion and
cultivated wills have been melded together by the
power of the Holy Spirit as we have sought and found
the will and purpose of God. God has produced a unity
here, and only He could do it.

How do we respond to growth and oneness of mind
like this? I am sure some people thought this was just
a case of a successful church, perhaps a product of the
leadership. But I knew something that others didn't
know. I knew that God was going to build this church
regardless. He didn't do it because of me. He did it
because He had decided to do it. I have never
forgotten that.

We formed a Facilities Planning Commission. It
became clear that we were called upon to build. This
was the leading of the Lord unitedly determined by
that commission after surveying the needs, then
voted by the vestry unanimously.

We prayed, asking, "How large a church should we
build?"

A word of wisdom was given to the senior warden
(Ed Leaton): "God has given us this property. We
should build the church as large as we can on this
property."

The architects proceeded. With many prayers we
took the plans to the Darien Planning and Zoning
Commission. Unanimously they rejected the plans,
saying they would constitute an overextensive use of
the property.

We knew, and this included the vestry and clergy, that they were right. We had somehow misheard the direction of the Lord.

The following Sunday I told the congregation that *God had led us to know that He had now and forever cut the umbilical cord tying this congregation to 471 Mansfield Avenue, Darien.* What God wants to do cannot be done exclusively on this property.

The Facilities Planning Commission went back to work, surveying every possibility of buying other land to build on, other buildings which could be purchased, merging with existing congregations. Only one church, St. John's in Stamford, was remotely large enough, but had insufficient parking facilities.

Finally, the commission made its formal recommendation to the vestry:

(1) That St. Paul's commit itself to *the building of the Living Church*, not a building to house St. Paul's Church.

(2) That we commit ourselves to *the use of public facilities*.

The words seemed clear enough, but what would they mean when applied practically?

The Living Church? That sounded good, but what did it mean?

How could a "set-apart" people possibly depend upon *public* facilities?

Fullam, still the patient man, spelled it out to any who might still be puzzled on Sunday, April 17. Bearing the alternating expressions of a man both relieved and excited, he stood in his long, off-white, Franciscan-styled robe, and shared the vision of the leadership. It was another of those unusual moments in the corporate life of

St. Paul's, a time when the atmosphere seemed to change, and the dark-brownness of the sanctuary furniture seemed to flake the air with a sort of goldenness. The stillness, pervasive, was utterly light.

St. Paul's is indeed called to build a church. But the church we are called to build is not of bricks and mortar. Rather we are called to build *the Living Temple*—the body of Christ.

Now the New Testament says the church is not a building anyway. The church is people. The church is the body of Christ, a living organism, and we are called of God as a parish to put all of the considerable resources of this parish behind the building of the church, *the Living Church*.

Now that has certain important consequences for us, for the church of Jesus Christ is the church that is spread out in all the world. It is not limited to the St. Paul's congregation, as we all know. We are to commit ourselves to the building of this wider church. Now you can say, of course, that that includes our people, such as God brings here—and that's true—*but the traditional boundaries that separate a local church from the wider church have just been erased by our God.*

Now that's going to require some radical rethinking—a complete revision of the way we think about the church. God is calling us to think about the wider church. This is the church of which we are a part. *It's the only church that Jesus founded.* It's the only church that has existed from the beginning to this very day, and it's the only church with the guarantee that the gates of hell will not prevail against it.

We need to learn then to look at the broader picture, to open our eyes up to the wider scope. Look at the way we've organized ourselves. Why, we have an Inreach Commission and an Outreach Commission. We spend part of our money—most of it—on ourselves; we spend a considerable amount on people outside our parish. That division will have to go; that whole way of thinking will have to go. We cannot draw the lines anywhere between *us* and *them*—because, you see, we are called to build *the church*.

Now, you say, "Well, where *is* the church?"

The church is wherever God's people are. And wherever God leads us—wherever He opens the door—we will follow in. I have a feeling that the building of the church will take this congregation around the world before we're done.

The second recommendation was this: that we positively commit ourselves to the use of public facilities. Obviously, we have to house this sprawling enterprise. But how do we do it?

If we want to have a parish dinner—and our parish is far too large to have a dinner here in this building—then we'll rent the Holiday Inn or some other place. Or if we want more offices then we can have in this building, then we can go down to an office building in Darien or somewhere around and rent such facilities. I can tell you, even at Darien prices, rent is a pittance compared to what we would pay in interest on the mortgage we were contemplating for the building of bricks and mortar.

This recommendation to use public facilities underscores the fact that the church is not a building. St. Paul's is wherever St. Paul's people are gathering to worship the Lord and praise Him. That is what we are called to do.

It means, of course, that we have to have a place

for our worship. We can't turn people away. We thought about it, prayed about it, and came to the united conclusion that there was really only one place around where we could do the job that had to be done in terms of worship of the people, and that was the high school.

So we went to the town and asked if the high school would be available for use on a regular basis, and we found out that it would be, in the fall. And the proposal is that we go then to the high school on a regular basis. Remember, it is not interim; it is not a trial thing at all. We've committed ourselves irrevocably to the use of such facilities as are available. If we outgrow the high school, well, there's always Madison Square Garden. But the point is, we look for where God would put us and where He opens doors. . . .

We have the opportunity to demonstrate the truth of what we believe, that the church is not a building and that it doesn't even depend upon a building; that God will be where His people gather; and that we are indeed a pilgrim people called to follow Him wherever He shall go.

The Facilities Planning Commission at the church had a third proposal, one that was less immediate in its outworking. When the church was constructed, the zoning regulations allowed for expansion of the sanctuary to seat 350 people. Recalling the word of wisdom given to Senior Warden Leaton—that they should build as large a facility as they could on their property—the commission members and the vestry agreed to take steps to modify the existing building to include 350 seats.

"But," emphasized Fullam, "this is not so that we can come back. Don't entertain that hope. But we need seating capacity for our weektime ministries. Look, we have a full church on Tuesdays and again on Wednesday nights, and we're often overextended at other times."

Additionally, of course, the plan for regular services at the high school included full use of the Mansfield Avenue property on Sundays for a youth church. God had called a St. Paul's layman, Gordon Jelliffe, to full-time service as coordinator of youth work, and that aspect of the ministry was only beginning to mushroom.

What Is God Doing?

With logistical matters falling into some sort of order, the people of St. Paul's Church, looking past the summer and into the fall, were wondering more than ever what God was doing to them—and why. Looking with them, Fullam helped find answers.

Some may have thought his words glib, maybe even pompous. Indeed, if one looks at transcriptions and reports of some of the things he said during that period, he could interpret them as too simplistic. But, during the soul-searchings of those days and weeks, there was no glibness or pomposity. The words and ideas—the understanding and the perception—did not merely glide into place. They came through sweat and tears, and fear of pride.

"We must all understand," Fullam said with wide-eyed humility, "that it is not because of us that God has chosen to do a good work here. It has to do with His sovereign purpose. We are an instrument in the hand of God. There's no question that it will be done, because God will not be interfered with. He never has and He won't. He said, 'This is something I am going to do in that place.' He is putting a body of people together who will be and are now responsive to His leading. We are certain, therefore, that God will guide us and perform what He has promised."

Going before the full congregation, Fullam shared his understanding of where the Lord was leading them in more practical terms. It was a view—a summary—in which they seemed to find unity.

Now we also have been praying that the Lord will sharpen our focus on what the ministry is that He is calling us to, and it seems to us that God is raising up a ministry with four central features.

First is that we are to be a *worshiping people*. The worship of this congregation is a major concern. We need to have *room* to do it and the *time* to do it. You will find that if you move along with the eternal God, He may not fit in with your schedule, and that means you need to change your schedule to fit Him, because He doesn't adapt to ours, you see.

Now this means further that the worship of the Lord will be a key part, as it has been, in the life of our congregation. There are people who come from miles around just to fellowship on Tuesdays and Sundays in this place because God is here and they know it. They may not understand too much about what is going on, but they sense the presence of the Lord, and we must never lose that. God sits enthroned on the praises of His people.[11]

We have tried to have a worship that is dignified and at the same time free, a service that has the liturgy of our church and so forth, but has the word and sacrament in good balance—where there is a balance between formality and informality, where people can be free to express themselves by raising their hands or genuflecting or making the sign of the cross or any other manual or physical way of expressing their faith, where people can be free to

___

[11]Psalm 22:3.

glory in the Lord, to love Him, and to worship and sing His praise. That's a major focus.

Secondly, God has shown us that this church must always be a *caring fellowship*. Now, it's exciting to worship with hundreds of people, but it's necessary for God's people also to have smaller places where they fit in. And God is showing us to give great attention to the pastoral needs of the congregation and all such as He leads to us.

And that would mean our extended families that God has been blessing and will no doubt increase. But more than that, people are turning to us for counsel and help—all kinds of people, from beyond the borders of this parish. We cannot say, if people out there are seeking our help, that we cannot help them. God won't let us do that. Anybody who comes to us for help, we can believe, God will raise up the ability of this congregation to meet it. That means we need a major counseling facility that will involve lay counselors, clerical counselors or clergy, and also professional counselors, perhaps medical doctors, psychologists and perhaps psychiatrists who are dedicated Christian people carrying on their ministries within that framework.

Now we fully expect when fall comes to launch a major effort in increased pastoral ministries, making it possible for everyone who seeks a place of fellowship to find it.

The third major thing about this church and its ministry is that we are ever to be a *center for teaching*. Now we have this reputation already to a large extent, but it must continue and even increase. You will never have mature Christians apart from teaching. Churches where they do not have teaching of the Word of God do not produce strong Christians because the Holy Spirit produces faith in reference to the Word. When the Word is taught, then the Spirit works, and then the people come to understand and grow—and that's really the key to the phenomenal growth of this church, not only numerically, but spiritually. It rests upon a sound foundation of teaching.

We are in a position to attract to this church the finest teachers in the Christian church worldwide, and we shall be doing that.

Also, you might say, what about this lovely facility where we are? What use will be put to that? Well, it will be the center of our operations, no doubt, but on Sundays this whole facility, we are expecting, will be a children's church. God has called us to put considerable effort and energy and prayer and dedication into the training of our children and the equipping of them as people. This will call for the very best we've got in every way, not only in terms of people and commitment, but in terms of resources.

I believe it will not be too long before people will come to St. Paul's and this fellowship simply because of the outstanding ministry to the children that we will have in this place—a ministry where you will see, where you are now sitting, a place filled with children praising the Lord and being instructed in the faith, where they will have a chance to grow together and understand the same principles that God is teaching us as adults. This facility here will be a children's church, and it is glorious, and I am looking forward to it.

The fourth area of our ministry is that we are called forever to be a *launching pad for ministries*. We have seen clearly that it is the will of God that all of His people exercise significant ministries—*all* of His people. And we are to bend every effort to facilitate that and help it to come to pass.

Jesus said, when you look to the world and see it is white unto harvest, pray that the Lord of the harvest will thrust forth laborers into the field.[12] And we are doing that and God is raising up in our midst men and women to whom He is giving ministries that we can recognize and then facilitate.

I suspect that one of the major uses of our money in the days ahead will be in making it possible for people to whom God has clearly given ministries to exercise those ministries on a full-time basis, if that seems to be the calling. This means, do not be surprised, if this church grows, that we add perhaps—not twenty more priests, but twenty more people from the congregation to serve full time, and that we support ministries that will build the Living Church—build the people of God—and create the kind of a congregation the Lord God wants in this place.

Some of you have already given a lot of money to the building fund. Maybe you're saying to yourself, well, since we're committed to the building of the Living Church, what about that money? Well, it looks like it's about enough—when all's been paid that's been pledged—to take care of the modifications of this building—we don't know. But I can tell you something. Do you know, it costs about thirty-eight cents to buy a single brick? One brick. And do you know that the New Testament says you and I are living bricks in the Temple of the Living God,[13] and of how much worth are those bricks? Jesus said, if a man gains the whole world and loses his soul, he's lost everything.[14] In the sight of God, the living bricks, each one, are worth more than the combined wealth of the entire world.

[12]John 4:35, Matthew 9:38.   [13]1 Peter 2:5.   [14]Mark 8:36.

So how much is it going to cost to build the Living Temple?

Everything you've got. Everything you've got.

We will need hundreds of thousands of dollars. What do we need it for? We need it to build the Living Temple. And let me tell you something—God will prosper you so that you can give in order that this ministry may be accomplished. It will take more than money. It will take the commitment of God's people in this place.

We have turned a corner. From now on, nothing will be the same. God has spoken, and by His grace we will move forward.

Of course, we have the trepidation that the children of Israel felt as they stood on the edge of the Promised Land. But we also have the same promise they had: "I will go with you and I will care for you."[15]

I call this whole congregation to rise before the Lord and accept that challenge. A church we will build, where moth and rust cannot corrupt, where thieves cannot break through and steal[16]—a church that will glorify the name of the Living God, turn multitudes of people from sin unto righteousness, and will be a light in the midst of darkness, life in the midst of death, joy in the midst of sorrow.

That is what we are called to, my dear people. It is a high and a holy calling. We do not deserve it. We were chosen because of the sovereign purpose of God upon us, and we shall not fail Him—because I know one thing about the Lord's speaking to me in reference to this: It wasn't conditional. He didn't say to me, "If you do this, this is what will happen." The zeal of the Lord of Hosts will accomplish this. God will not let anybody, or any person, or any group of people stand in the way. It will be done. It will be

---

[15]Joshua 1:2-5.   [16]Matthew 6:19-20.

264

done because it's the determined purpose of Almighty God to do a mighty work for the restoring of the church. Praise God that He has seen fit to make us a part of that great calling.

I want to ask you to go to prayer with me now. We'll take a moment of silence first. But then I want to ask you to join in prayer, all over the congregation. As the Lord moves you, let us pray for this great and holy calling that God has placed upon us. Let us rededicate ourselves to this task. Let the Lord fill us with that peace that comes from finding His will and dedicating ourselves to it, and the joy that comes from obedience.

The Lord be with you. Let us pray.

Epilogue

I suppose an epilogue is a device invented by some writer who simply didn't know how to end his story. That suits me perfectly, it seems. For there is no ending for the miracle in Darien. It may only be in the preliminary stages, in fact, or it may be far advanced. But it is certain that it has not concluded.

Similar, yet different, such miracles are also in varying stages throughout the country. To write about them would require a scope that this story was not designed to accommodate and would only make the problem of ending that much more difficult.

As for Darien, the growth in ministry at home and abroad runs ahead of any reporter's efforts to pin it down; the progress toward genuine Christian fellowship ebbs and flows, then surges again in quantity and quality far too profound to be uncovered; the healings of individuals, couples, and families are too numerous to be tabulated.

And there are uncertainties. Will the Mansfield Avenue facility be expanded to cope with mid-week activity, or will municipal regulation mandate a new course? Will God continue the growth, or will He establish a plateau and move in other directions? Will twentieth-century people—even thoroughly committed Christian people—be able to break the bonds of rugged individualism completely and live fully in the fellowship called for in ancient Scripture?

Regardless of the answers to these questions, regardless of what God chooses to do in that rare little suburban town in southern Connecticut where He has already done so much, we have the assurance of the Lord himself that He will build His universal church—"and the powers of death shall not prevail against it."

Now to him who by the power at work within us is able to do far more abundantly than all that we ask or think, to him be glory *in the church* and in Christ Jesus to all generations, for ever and ever. Amen.

Ephesians 3:20-21.